Neurogenesis

Wolfgang Pauli and the Long Road to Damascus

Art, Science, Creativity,

and the Role of Entropy in Self-Realization

by David Courtney

Neurogenesis

Introduction

Neurogenesis

IT'S TOO LATE TO TURN THE OTHER CHEEK

I wasn't big on living where big snakes, and rhinos and lions roam at large. It was this fear that kept me from running off to Africa to be a missionary. Certainly when I gave my heart to the Lord I knew the small print declared that I would go where God wanted me to go. I would do his work. As a young man I could be deeply touched and simultaneously conflicted deep within my conscience. I could be touched and moved.

Now as an adult I'm rather frightened by those who want to sock it to you, in the name of the Lord. I firmly believe that any organization becomes a hierarchical interpersonal reality. God has little say in the matter. People being people do what people do: move God out of the picture. The Israelites are archetypal here. Moses no sooner heads up the mountain than the people turn their backs on God preferring a golden calf, something of their own construction. Man worships himself.

Tonight I watched a forensics show. Two college sweethearts were living the American dream. They were married with two children and lived in a beautiful house. Both were active in the church. The wife taught Bible study.

It turns out she was having an affair with a macho guy. She and macho guy would kill her husband in cold blood and head for Mexico.

Who are we under the skin of things? How twisted are we?

Priests who abuse altar boys resist being touched by the belief system they ritualize. How can a person stand in a church and be such a sinner? People's brains are so looped they can ignore certain information and do it routinely. The preacher's wife didn't take the Bible to heart, especially not *Thou Shalt not Kill*. Gatekeepers of the gas chambers, usually the local citizenry, didn't question the jobs they had either. Hannah Arendt describes Eichmann as a normal Joe. The banality of evil was her phrase to show how untouched a man could be when sending trainloads of people to the gas chambers. He had a point when he said if he objected, he would lose his job. At a nearby hospital a surgery head went into surgical operations with blood splattered boots. He would make crude jokes etc. I see this as similar. Everyone defers to power. Nobody called this cowboy surgeon on it for years. To stand up for right even when it is the right thing to do entails repercussions. Still, it is excruciating to think of this stuff against a moral backdrop.

Philip Seymour Hoffman played a gasoline-sniffing addict in a movie yet failed to address his own addiction. The history of the human race is pivotal here. Because we have no conscience and are benumbed by information, we cannot be touched. We cannot be moved. We've lost our bearings and our scruples. We have no answer for the media bombarded world we live in. We fake it. We move through life within its parameters, rarely probing what we are declaring about ourselves through our actions. Quotations from *The Catcher in the Rye* paint a pretty good portrait of modern developments. We became fakes and phoneys by not taking notice of ourselves. When people 'make it' they forget where they came from. What they do is put their lives on cruise control forgetting about who they once were. The mechanism by which we forget who we were is a primary mover in taking us where we are going. Where we are going is not a place. It is a speed. In a media-inundated world our bombarded brains displace old information with new information continuously. This displacement speed is our attention span quotient. If we unplug waves of boredom make us feel disconnected and dead.

NEUROGENESIS

One strand of argument in Neurogenesis is this: Normalization is bad for our mental health. Too many things pass through us and void large areas of the collective conscience. We are so accepting of our socialization that we obscure, often intentionally, the issues around our demise. We go through life acting or acting out, passing ourselves off as, what else: NORMAL. Normal is a virus. Normalization prevents you from maintaining human character traits thereby separating you from your true identity. I want to draw up a picture of the alienation built into normalization. Bell's Let's Talk Day is today (January 30) and so much lip service and pomp and ceremony go into it that people can't see what we are doing to ourselves in creating a false sense of security. The way it is currently handled is not wonderful for mental health. Many mental illness sufferers of depression or whatever knows the mind can mess up. It can become a trap. Dealing with mental illness, they have had their eyes opened. Many individuals point to a traumatic event as life-changing for the better.

I've had a couple life-changing events (depression, back issue). When you go through hell for a heavenly cause you feel transformed.

Leaf's coach Mike Babcock's advice... lean on someone; go to our friends and supporters for support; if you don't have anyone, get help professionally. Supporting in the simplest terms the status quo criteria undermines the nature of mental health by reducing complexity to simplicity.

Neat and tidy. Mike Babcock believes his players who want it will rise to the top, if I remember correctly his earlier statements. He doesn't realize that the will to succeed involves levels of psychological comfortability with the challenge. It's not just a bunch of animals attacking a carcass where appetite dictates success.

What does one give up by becoming a success? And 15 years later retiring from the sport, where are you likely to be emotionally? Psychology and interpersonal transitional reality are more important to some players than others. Some like it hard and fast and straight-up. Others realize there is no straight-up. By not having intuitive, conceptual, empathic people talking about mental health issues, we are left with the stupid proposition that a sport has an answer. Sports can change lives but often loses ground as individual ages.

That answer to any locker room question includes involvement in an erroneous self-concept. The object is not to get along with others and phony up. That's the problem. Members of the herd think group think works for the better. The fact is it separates one from one's values. That's why we can look back at one of the most insightful investigations of anxiety and depression ever. *The Catcher in the Rye* is such a document. Everybody everywhere, except for maybe Allie and Phoebe, have been contaminated by a culture desperately in need of healing. Everyone is snowed under my Normalization.

"I kept trying to picture my mother or somebody, or my aunt, or Sally Hayes' crazy mother, standing outside some department store and collecting dough for people in a beat-up old

straw basket. It was hard to picture. Not so much my other, but those other two. My aunt's pretty charitable – she does a lot of Red Cross work and all – but she's very well-dressed and all, and when she does anything charitable she's always very well dressed and has lipstick on and all that crap. I couldn't picture her doing anything for charity if she had to wear black clothes and lipstick while she was doing it. And old Sally Hayes' mother. Jesus Christ. The only way she could go around with a basket collecting dough would be if everybody kissed her ass for her when they made a contribution," (The Catcher in the Rye, p. 114 J D SALINGER)).

"You ought to go to a boys' school sometime …. It's full of phonies, and all you do is study so that you can learn enough to be smart enough to be able to buy a goddam Cadillac, and you have to keep making believe you give a damn if the football team loses, and all you do is talk about girls and liquor and sex all day, and everybody sticks together in these dirty little goddam cliques," (The Catcher in the Rye, p. 131).

We sabotage ourselves because we lack introspection. Holden held a mirror up to a cultured stuffed full of itself.

We fill our heads with the colloquial and the simplistic. Boys will be boys.

In my maturing process I've come to see ambition in a bad light. Marc Antony, referring to Julius Caesar, said, **"If ambition is a grievous fault then grievously has Caesar paid."** Caesar's ambition was to be King. Brutus and Cassius, his peers, would make Caesar pay the ultimate price for his ambition, by stabbing him in the back.

The words, 'et tu Brute,' echo through history and refer to Caesar looking at his 'friend' Brutus and saying, and you? Having friends stab us in the back or pepper our body full of holes is what all the forensic shows detail. If you watch these shows it shows how screwed up normal looking people are. Phoniness is mainstream. A lot of people can get away with it, with passing themselves off as normal as the girl next door. People in nice houses with white picket fences go stark raving mad and kill, kill, kill. Because phoniness is mainstream; it is so much part of us we have trouble seeing it. It is somehow integrated.

An ambition to sell a lot of books is an ego-ambition. To make money is an ego ambition. A successful, book, I assume outfits the writer in a shining countenance. A successful writer doesn't have to knock on doors. Doors open automatically.

That is not my ambition. My ambition is to point out how the very act of NORMALIZATION is the root of most mental health issues. Existentialist writers have said as much but now neuroscience in respect of brain plasticity says the same. The quest is firing and wiring a resilient brain. The most resilient brain is a happy brain. A repressed brain can be problematic. A repressed brain can blow its stack. The repressed identity can become a rat backed into a corner and ready to lash out.

When your perception field and your perception are one you operate in a prescriptive pre-cognition realm of mind. You live in a bubble. I've seen the title, *Cloudy with Meatballs*, somewhere. That could describe a picture of the human mind. There are islands of succinctness against a backdrop of vagueness. This allows people to be phony even when they least think they are phony.

Wolfgang Pauli was king of the Physics World. He set out on the long road to Damascus because he wasn't happy with his mind and his soul. What his story speaks volumes about is the carefulness of Science to remain transfixed by materialism while ignoring the human mind. Planck, Pauli, Jung and Alfred North-Whitehead, among others, see the mind, the psyche, as a molecular force in the material world. These are big names. Normalized Science doesn't go there because, as Einstein said, Scientists like to hammer nails through the easiest and thinnest part of reality.

Art could save us but Art has lost sight of Creativity and Originality. Curators and managers are beguiled, corrupted fundamentally in their perception. Why?

Because Art is a business forced to play business games. Its bureaucracy is an organization of sell-outs, systemic parasites sucking blood from a dead carcass. Enshrined with academia, they suffer the effects of their own ideation, their own in-breeding. This is particularly unfortunate because sustenance of one's mentality depends on accessing fluidity primarily concerning neuroplasticity and neurogenesis. Art puts its finger on the pulse of the Sublime. We need Art to break on through to the other side, to throw off the shackles of Normalization. The handlers, the high priests or, as Vincent called them, the

Pharisees of Art, are fakes. This is both ironic and sad that ART as facilitator of vision is distorter of vision. Art has lost its way.

This book, NEUROGENESIS is exemplary of synchronicity. I was working on a book about Metaphorical Thinking when this book emerged. It was like the one book had given birth to another book. You'll forgive me, I hope, for using a metaphor to set the stage for Neurogenesis.

ANTHILL - THE YOUNG AND THE RESTLESS

Have you ever studied an anthill? An anthill is alive like one organism and ants traverse the terrain carrying loads 2 or 3 times their size. And they are organized like pyramid slaves. Every detail of their reality is in this overall functional-ism. If you've watched ants on an anthill you know their patterns are pretty succinct. Everyone knows their jobs and there are no confrontations. They get on with it. They are compliant to this larger entity the anthill. The anthill rules.

One day in ant-land an ant named Ezekiel, not the one from the Cowboys, roams to the top of a branch. Ezekiel has an idea. Sacrificing his life to this mundane repetitive existence has been difficult and the more he thinks about it the less appealing it is. What kind of life is this he asks himself? One day he extricates himself from the scene and heads cross country. Eventually he pulls up in a space that seems safe. In a couple years he has a wonderful deck and a great view. Now and again he remembers his fellow ants and how mindlessly entrenched they were in what they were doing. It was like they were hypnotized by their routines.

It was certainly not easy. There was mud and rainfall and unfamiliar terrain. Many times Ezekeil was on the brink of giving up. But he was happy. The hardship was worth it.

The history of the human race is a history of bloodshed and failure. Civilizations get so far then they self-destruct over the same old stuff: power-mongering and sandbox aggression. Normalization is an imprinting patterning process. It is powerful and inherent in just about everything we do. The themes within the normalization process congeal in fire and wire habits that script precognition and preclude change. Standing up against uniformity and normalization is increasingly important. The more wayward and irretrievable the mental dispositions of the collective mind the more the urgency.

The most relevant archetypal proposition is reflected in the Biblical story of Lot and his journey out of Sodom and Gomorrah. Lot has to turn his back on everything and everyone, so pervasive is the degeneracy, so thematic and irreconcilable, is the popular milieu. Lot's wife can't resist taking one last look at the familiar metropolis. Sodom and Gomorrah, soon to be a bonfire of vanity.

As she turns into a pillar of salt we see that God isn't kidding around. This is serious. There have been many humans throughout history who have taken on the sins of the world. When somebody like Socrates comes along, they kill him. When somebody like Jesus comes along they crucify him. Ditto for Malcolm X, Gandhi and Martin Luther King Jr., who left us by way of bullets. We don't like somebody who questions where we are going. Particularly when, wherever we are going, we are going there fast. Like now.

We, as humans, are reduced to being an information bundle. How does an information bundle self-correct? How do you stem the tide? How do you put your finger in the dyke? Chaos seems to be gaining the upper hand. Entropy seems a force at work. Things human fall apart.

Like Apostle Paul and physicist, Wolfgang Pauli, I had my Damascus moment. I had identified Entropy as an 'enemy' concept. Entropy was the enemy that I was getting ready to persecute. But turns out, it isn't an enemy anymore. I see it in the light of a new contextual arrangement, an arrangement I favour. Thinking of entropy as energy (dissipating structures) is so elegant. We plug into the sublime. The sublime is chaos or all energy. We draw on its power. We recycle entropy.

There is nothing so imprisoning than an irrevocable or non-reversible position. We can change our minds, we can migrate firing and wiring into a different order of being. We can save ourselves from Normalization.

Like a Black Hole or a giant vacuum cleaner, Entropy seems to feast on discord and dismantle coherence. It is probably visualized more advantageously as a hole in things. The gap where there is the spectrum of everything, the whole periodic table, and beyond. Everything. Like white noise. Like white noise covering the noise spectrum, entropy-energy fosters a diffusion rate across the spectrum. Infinity and eternity. There is a paradox.

The colossal opportunism that comes about when old solid state structures are blown away is the reciprocal and recyclable advantage of Entropy. A confrontation with Entropy can plug the self into the sublime. Energy is neither created nor destroyed. Energy equals mass. Mass equals energy. The reciprocal advantage of plugging into chaos suggests sustainable interminable energy. Creativity goes on and on. It's what Creation is about. It sources through neurogenesis.

Entropy is the quickening. This entails a sublimation process of enormous potential. Epiphany is not out of the question. No recognizable physical laws exist in entropy. It is the absence of structure and antithetical to definition. Numbers spin out of control creating hyperbole, a world beyond probability cycles.

How we amplify time and space is part of our divergence trajectory. Spots of time like rabbit holes could lead to somewhere -- not like here, not like where we are. If we could go like Alice into a Wonderland then what?

Andre Breton saw this point of contact, this breakthrough moment, as accessing the sublime, the point between. It is the place between life and death, up and down, and it moves us from here to there. It is at this point we get in the gap, between past and future. We confront the self as the in-between. It is there we make of ourselves what we will.

One has to psychologically work out one's position of freedom. It is individualistic. This positioning is the most difficult thing because the 'point sublime' is a figment of one's intuitive imagination but none the less real for all of that.

"We would say that the conscious and unconscious railways each comprise a myriad of densely interconnected lines, and that the two systems are also connected to each other at various points …. The human sensory system

sends the brain about eleven million bits of information each second …. The actual amount of information we can handle has been estimated to be somewhere between sixteen and fifty bits per second," (Leonard Mlodinow, Subliminal, p. 33).

You have a lot going around and around in your brain continuously. Finding the points of connection with the sublime is what true creative Art is all about. The bridge is the right modality. Access is important because eventually under the regime and thought structure of Normalization we lose the access to the unconscious.

Original exploration connected to the essence of transposition, transformation and transcendence, is embodied in this notion of creativity. Creativity is Neurogenesis and Neuroplasticity in action.

Most excitingly, maybe any Humpty-human being can be put back together by his own volition. Entropy might be the embodiment of the absolute, the unknown author of Kundalini, and the arbitrator of Karma. In a sense we create our own brains.

SCHOOL DAZE

Like ants in the anthill, our organized realities avoid the big picture. We get by without taking the hard look that self-evaluation requires. Much is routinized beyond question. Nowhere is this more evident than in our schools. I recently had the opportunity to ask a couple of school board superintendents about statistics regarding medicated students. They suggested that a compilation of such records might be considered an invasion of privacy and hence no such lists exist.

This makes education a game of blind man's bluff. Our education system is riddled with inadequacies. Our answer is to superimpose the past on the present, pretending that it's business as usual. The foundational strategies of learning are strategies that quickly lose their way in the upending techno blizzard. A bird's eye view means facilitating what we need to hold onto and what we need to let go of. When we lose access to the sublime we lose access to the self-correcting motifs that keep us mentally reliant. Treating ourselves as information hard drives misses essence criteria. Art necessarily challenges the techno reality that by default establishes the mental illness epidemic. Being creative reflects a self different than a 'downloaded' self.

We fail to acknowledge the problem of personalization, however clear and present the danger. Normalization depersonalizes us and leaves us with nothing to hang onto.

THE ART OF THE DEAL

A report from Switzerland today paints a sad picture of a culture twisted and capsizing. Prince William, at an economic summit in Davos, Switzerland, tried to enlist celebrities for a Heads Up initiative regarding mental illness. Heads Up wants to erase the stigma. The Prince couldn't get even one celebrity to sign on. Einstein in Berlin authored a petition concerning the growth of Nazi propaganda and anti-Semitism. Einstein could get only one signature. Just one!

We live in a time where people are too often value-less and soul-less and unwilling to differentiate and grow. Ted Bundy, as gruesome a mass murderer as there has been, had attractive groupies following the goings-on in the testimony at his trials. People were fascinated. He became a Star. The Press called him an All-American charmer, the boy next door etc.

Co-author of *The Art of The Deal*, who should therefore know Trump, calls Trump a heartless, soul-less sociopath. Also very all-American.

Surely Bell, being a media company, could easily generate a few news reels on where the money is going and why we should be encouraged. If they did I'd sleep better. I can line up a lot of people to testify to Bell's and Roger's stonewalling on issues. Hypocrisy is foundational in White Society. The almighty buck triumphs.

Because of Blue Monday etc. there are documentaries on sleep studies on TV tonight. Losing sleep cooks the brain. There isn't the absorption of learning in the sleep cycles and tension can be a daily challenge. One can function with a lot of sleep debt without recognizing how it's all going down. None of these documentaries, other than giving a mere nod to meditation and relaxation, reflect on the psychologies that cause sleeplessness. Sleeplessness comes from unconscious and subconscious turmoil, not from having a bad mattress. Depression comes from psychological issues not as some claim, from gut bacteria.

Throughout my writing I try to use quotations as benchmarks to co-ordinate thinking which remains a challenging thing to do in uncertain times is. You can check me out by chasing the associative information regarding my sources.

We develop our self-concept by our attention span for various things. These things reflect back who we are.

Where do you stand in relation to the idea of Soul? Of course you don't think about it.

"One way of getting at this feature is in terms of the notion of self-interpretation. A fully competent human agent not only has some understanding (WHICH MAY BE ALSO MORE OR LESS MISUNDERSTANDING), of himself, but is partly constituted by this understanding……..TO BE A FULL HUMAN AGENT, TO BE A PERSON OR A SELF IN THE ORDINARY MEANING, IS TO EXIST IN A SPACE DEFINED BY DISTINCTIONS OF WORTH," (Charles Taylor, Human Agency and Language, p. 3-4).

Distinctions of worth come from jumping through the hoops of the system. This is not true worth simply because the system generationally operates within erroneous preconditions. This means growing up with co-ordinate measurements that determine our social distinction. We clear the hurdles and we get patted on the back. 'My, how tall you are getting.'

Agency involves seeing the self as part of the backdrop and distinguishing from there. Backdrop is too often indivisible from who we are.

"Perhaps these have been given authoritatively by the culture more than they been elaborated in the deliberation of the person concerned, but they are his in the sense that they are incorporated into his self-understanding, in some degree and fashion. My claim is that this is not just a contingent fact about human agents, but is essential to what we would understand as full, normal human agency …. Our personhood cannot be treated scientifically in exactly the same way we approach our organic being. What it is to possess a liver or a heart is something I can define quite independently in the space of questions in which I exist for myself, but not what it is to have a self or be a person," (Charles Taylor, Human Agency and Language, p. 3-4)

It is central and not contingent within human agency that we essentially address essence needs. Nothing is more central than leaving our personal signature. It is how we make ourselves who we are. Art can be how we approach our own mental contours and ideation biases. The attempt to plug in to the sublime, which is the source of inspirational magic, is the essence of Art. What art always needs is something more original, more meaningful and hence more daring. Thinking outside the box is letting the imagination roam beyond the ordinary. When Society systemically keeps a Art on a short leash we lose the ability to taste freedom.

Here is part of a letter from Vincent Van Gogh to his sister.

"I have a study of a garden, almost a metre wide…I know very well not a single flower was drawn, that they're just little licks of colour, red, yellow, orange, green, blue, violet, but the impression of all those colours against one another is nonetheless there in the painting as in Nature. However, I imagine it would disappoint you and appear ugly were you to see it," (Bernadette Murphy, Van Gogh's Ear, p. 105).

The future of painting needs to look ugly. Ugly is something outside our normalized assimilation process. We need practice in bearing witness to the Normalization dissimilation apparatus, to be able to arrive at a fresh vista. It's not easy. It doesn't come with a job description. Divergence, dissociation and dislocation are features of our existence, something we can't make sense of without effort. We can't make sense of it with everyday levels of discourse. We often can't even distill it into words. What passes for Art in local Art groups is colouring in the lines of convention and derivative of a longstanding tradition of blindness. Making expectation definitive and the experience routine negates the potentiation of creative awareness. The types of mind processing are antithetical, one to the other. In cash register art there is no catharsis, no enlargement of the soul.

Jung and Pauli were not on the same page when it came to Jesus Christ. Pauli saw the archetypal compass of the soul as necessarily manifest before Christ. What I mean by this is based on seeing evolution as approaching greater levels of civilization. To get there you can't despise your neighbour; you have to love your neighbour. This is agape love, a principle of love: Live and let be.

Loving one another in the abstract is necessary to arrive at the security whereby we can live divergent lives without fear. Leonard Cohen says in his songs two important reflections.

I have seen the Future it is murder

Love is the only engine of survival.

I believe this too. Many religions incorporate the motifs that also are represented in motifs for healthy flexible plasticity. This is why Pauli sees the elements as pre-Christian. Evolutionary structures lead us to Christ's beliefs. Christ epitomizes love. **No greater love has a man than he lay done his life for another. All religions have a core of love. Then the church hierarchy covers up love with commandments about all sorts of things. People divide. Wars happen. Human kind seems incapable of moving on.**

I believe in the Gospel of Brain Plasticity. It is real and because of it, absolute conversion is possible. That said, the best we can do is elevate our firing and wiring to become more considerate, more wholesomely personalized self-aware individuals. Plasticity is God. It reflects God's grace. It is our salvation because it saves us from ourselves being less than we could be. For those of us left, an ever-dwindling number, consciousness requires of us the recognition that change happens. Change is integral neuroplasticity and neurogenesis.

"That which is called Christian Religion existed among the ancients, and never did not exist, from the beginning of the race until Christ came in the flesh, at which time the true religion which already existed began to be called Christianity," Saint Augustine (Robert B. Clarke, An Order Outside Time, p. 1).

Wolfgang Pauli, like Vincent Van Gogh was an individual who had to individuate. He had to be the person he needed to be. The adventure was in the becoming.

In so many ways we are out of control. Two nights ago parents (30 of them) were involved in a brawl during a hockey game. Everybody is carrying around a great deal of repression and subliminal angst. The truck driver who crashed into a bus full of hockey players in Saskatchewan did not intend to do what he did. Of intent he is innocent. Lots of people have run stop signs without crashing into something. This is an accident of time and place. That he is brown skinned and crashed into a bus full of hockey players is unfortunate. People want him to pay big time. He did not intend to kill those young men, not in his wildest dreams. The hate we conjure up for people we don't know is very Orwellian. It is often contrived by the media exploiting our repressed anger issues.

Neurogenesis is about the journey. Often times we have to take important steps to salvage ourselves. Dislocation can lead to dissociation. The self can disintegrate. And that can make for the Phoenix archetype--a self rising from its own ashes. It is becoming increasingly clear that a flexible mind with resourcefulness in the areas of neuroplasticity and neurogenesis is necessary for mental health. We are complex individuals and the highways and bi-ways of the mind are infinite. Infinity however gives way to Normalization. Normalization, pre-packages who we are supposed to be. We become wrapped up in our finite selves, and looking objectively and scientifically we miss the boat. Reduced to a mortal coil physical self, a self crippled and polarized by stresses we are ill at ease. Dis-ease happens because of the tension in our daily agenda, the daily grind.

Neurogenesis can save us when we become a hazard to ourselves.

I do have my wits enough about me to recognize that without my wife Christina this book wouldn't exist.

She'd be the first to tell you this. And it's absolutely true. It's a good thing she is the love of my life.

She also talked me out of getting personal about my personal fall out with the Art establishment. I dropped some DVDs along with my two books: *Theory of Mind* and *The Art of Sanity* at The Museum in Kitchener. I was encouraged to do so.

When I enquired of the curator down the road, she said she was too busy. She was curating a show in the Fall. Meanwhile I dropped the package off during March Break. Next month they will have been there a year. I dropped stuff off at Theatre

Orangeville because I wrote a play, *Screen* (in *The Art of Sanity*). My e-mails and phone calls for me to pick the stuff went unanswered. Again I was told face to face at Theatre Orangeville to drop it off. It costs money for a little guy to self-publish.

I joined Elora Art Group recently and dropped off a DVD. I had done this several years before, a few times. I never received a Thank You but No Thanks. Ditto now that I am a member. I find the Art establishment ignorant and rude. They should not have government grant support. They provide no worthwhile role in the community. They block true creative endeavour.
I could go on and on but my wife told me not to.
In contrast, my wife, who taught 16 Julys in Paris teaching Canadian students French, dropped a disc off at the world famous Le Pompidou. They sent me a letter!

I want to thank Caversham Booksellers in Toronto, and Booklore in Orangeville for putting my books on their shelves. K-W Bookstore not only puts them on the shelf right out front, the owner gives me lots of encouragement. Thanks.

Vivamus ut viximus - Let us be truthful to one another.

Neurogenesis

**Wither is fled the visionary gleam? Where
is it now, the glory and the dream?
Our birth is but a sleep and a forgetting:
The Soul that rises with us, our life's Star,
    Hath had elsewhere its setting,
        And cometh from afar:
    Not in entire forgetfulness,
    And not in utter nakedness,
But trailing clouds of glory do we come**

(Intimations of Immortality from Recollections of Early Childhood, Wordsworth)

Neurogenesis

Neurogenesis

Wolfgang Pauli and the Long Road to Damascus

Art, Science, Creativity,

and the Role of Entropy in Self-Realization

Neurogenesis

I think it important to characterize at the outset the nature of the discussion. Neurogenesis examines the status of mind structures and the role of brain plasticity in altering those structures. Beyond that it tries to isolate features of Normalization that work against us. We humans prefer reasoning built on illogical premises and that's because Normalization dishes up such reasoning every day.

Part of this distinction involves our definitive sense about numbers. When a doctor asked me on a scale of 1-10 where my pain threshold was at, she thought we were communicating. By giving it a number, 3 or 9 or whichever, we presumptuously delude ourselves about what we are communicating. We foster an artificial language and presume on its premises. We lose touch with certain realities in favour of other realities.

In *Spontaneous Healing* by Andrew Weil, pain is profiled as something complex and personal. Some go so far as to say pain is something in your head, something remembered and neurologically processed, and not real in the body. We all can relate to a 1-10 scale, however ridiculous the built-in assumptions in translating subjectivity. When it comes to pain like so much else one individual's floor is another individual's ceiling. This is just one example of how we contrive the conversation in favour of certain understandings.

The main concept to be deliberated upon is Normalization and how it erodes the mind curling up used-less axons and dendrites. This is why the mind backs up on itself. Mental health issues are everywhere. The fact is people are losing their minds at an astonishing rate.

Psychedelic drugs offer an opportunity to describe minds at work, particularly the mind structures in an act of a human being losing touch. The breakdown into a distorted dysfunctional normalized mind is everywhere apparent. Collectively a lot of people run aground while trying to keep the ship afloat. Psychedelics reveal the goings on within mind identification. Unfortunately any drug that doesn't come from a Pharmacy is suspect and in the case of psychedelics, demonized.

Another concept central to neurogenesis is how in losing touch with others we lose touch with ourselves, our own bodies even. The body keeps score. The mind carries forward.

My wife and I bought tap shoes recently because I want my brain to connect to the sounds through my body. Toes and neglected parts of the body can lose degrees of connection with the central nervous system.

Objective detachment has always been the battle cry of Science. Wolfgang Pauli and others see Science as woefully trapped in a mind-game paradigm that pre-empts their ability to explore' themselves' in relation to

Science. If they could do this, they would see the dimensionality of things and apprehend that which is quantifiable and that which is not.

For Neurogenesis my core emphasis is on brain plasticity. Neurogenesis can birth a new self, with better and deeper resources than both Science and Normalization accounts for. This is a thinking cap book that will alter your mind as you read it.

We have different minds we can apply to our lives. When I deal with logistics or my taxes I want a mind that is creditable that can figure things out. There is a right answer and innumerable wrong answers. When I deal with Imagination I don't want to be creditable. I want to be free from credibility.

For logistics I need to thread the needle. There is no getting around it. For imagination I need a hole in the wall. When creative I need to let my logistics mind lapse because it is short-sighted. Also the cognitive mind is highly critical of any deviance and doesn't recognize when it is in over its head. Not everything fits like two plus two, and most emphatically not in the creative realm where incongruity and dissonance have a place. Not everything is quantifiable. Why is this of crucial importance? Brain gym games stress cognitive speed in recognizing and reacting to data absorption. They exercise association skills.

These are not what you need and not what your brain needs. Such cognition is the very cognition overemphasized in Normalization. What you need is a broader waveband of information like a creative endeavour. Only then do you have the wingspan required by a complex mind. To focal point your mind in these exercises discredits your brain because part of it sees such mental gymnastics as unnecessary friction. A mind at ease does not have to be responsible to bearing down on associative Rubrics.

All that said I have unearthed something worthy of a Science Fiction novel. I have come to believe that Normalization plays us false. By preventing encounters with the subconscious and the unconscious our consciousness fails to establish the appropriate depth. It's as if Aliens have sent Earthlings weird Cuba –like soundwaves and pulverized their thinking. We have been turned into stupefied automatons. Confronting the unconscious was the thematic discipline in the lives of Wolfgang Pauli and Carl Jung. For them it was all too evident how the psyche gets tangled up in false propositions.

My startling revelation is this: Normalization causes insanity. It's like we are made to want inferior lives because our brains are invaded with the thematic urges of the age we live in. We want to be normal when Normal is increasingly a consciousness-liability. When your mom said to you, If all your friends jumped off a cliff, would you? As far as the collective mind goes the answer is a resoundingly yes. We have bought into the packaging. The trouble with the human race is their preoccupation with how they look rather than what they represent archetypically. The dressing mirror dictates how they deck themselves out. This makes them fall for every trick in the book. They would rather be tricked than face off with themselves. Think about these three quotations.

"The present tendency to destroy all tradition or render it unconscious could interrupt the normal process of development for several hundred years and substitute an interlude of barbarism ... a predominantly scientific and technological education, such as is the usual thing nowadays, can also bring about a spiritual regression and a considerable increase of psychic dissociation," (C.J. Jung, Aion: Researches into the Phenomenology of the Self).

"That's the reason they're called lessons, the Gryphon remarked: because they lesson from day to day," (Lewis Carroll, Alice's Adventures in Wonderland).

"A business mentality may well be useful in a variety of social settings in the modern world. In

general ... it deflects tension from the intellectual needs of students, fosters savage competition that inhibits educational collaboration, and it focuses personal energies in largely inappropriate directions .... Students are trained to accept what is given and to minimize confrontations with the established order in all academic fields .... Over a period of four or more years, certain habits of mind and patterns of behaviour develop .... What these students learn above all is a subtle process of adaptation .... Their academic degrees signify a mere ability to persist in an organizational environment for a substantial period of time .... More than ever before, society demands men and women who are unafraid of taking risks and of questioning established policies," (Stillborn Education: A Critique of the American Research University, Paul Von Blum, University Press of America, Inc., 1986, pp. 14-15.

When you are highly associated you have a predisposition for your typology of association. You operate from a basis of the dots so far connected.

Neurogenesis is a piece of writing bent on tackling the big issues of the day concerning Art and Science and the future of humanity. Science and Art have different trajectories but arrive at the same place. Everything loses itself in the information jungle. Everything gets catalogued by hierarchy and sociology.

Existential questions are the very questions we collectively shy away from, tucked away as they are in the 'pace' of participation. The mesmerizing digitality around us has no time or space for offering legitimacy to such profoundly legitimate questions. One moment replaces the next with such speed, a sense of continuum and development is threatened. When continuum with its developmental milestones is threatened, coherence is threatened.

Modern trends eclipse all else. As time goes on, and it only takes a generation or two, for the attention span to change dramatically. Captivated by trivial pursuits and attention-grabbing contrivance, the brain fires and wires an irreducible lost-ness inside the hyperspace.

Hyper-dissociation becomes rampant. Benchmarks are historical anachronisms with no currency in a world overturned by technology. We ring around the rosy then we all fall down.

BUNK

Orwell said in *1984* that History is Bunk. History starts and stops with the regime and the contours of 'allowed' experience.. Experience is bracketed. Regardless of what the world tells us, we remain responsible for the species, each and every one of us. IS-NESS is immediately GONE-NESS and life is over before it starts. And that lack of presence in our own affairs distances us in every way from the understandings we need to survive mentally.

In essence we live our lives earning a living that never gets lived. This plays havoc in the mind. Down the stretch the body and mind start questioning the certainties that are no longer certain.

I am trying to confront the notion of thinking, of thought processes and the structure and capacity of the collective and individual mind. The role of the brain in apprehending reality is totally different than just a hundred years ago.

My use of quotations throughout is a way of triangulating the information in a world where fake news, dirty tricks, and outright lies become political platforms and published as truth. Never before has the necessity for being wary of one's sources been such high priority. One can look up a scientific study and dig a little deeper to see the pharmacies distorting information to their benefit.

I've intuitively written like Wittgenstein in his blue notebook. I studied Wittgenstein's *Philosophical Investigations* at York University. Normal paragraphs in Wittgenstein give way to utterances. I believe these utterances are easier to absorb precisely because they contradict the Normalization inherent in language and thought structures. Part of the 'normal' we need to look at includes basic grammar and arithmetic and how much they crutch our understandings.

We need to ask: where would our minds be without grammar and arithmetic? Grammar and arithmetic are storied structures in our brains. They were put there through usage. Like McLuhan did in the *Medium is the Massage* I'm trying to challenge and disrupt the normal frame-up of information transmission. Paragraphs give way to what I'm calling information quanta. The organizational principles are different. The arrangement in the brain is different.

I am throughout following the Science 'motif' because I want to break through to Science. I want to inform Science that it possesses certain psychological tendencies (tragic flaws) and these tendencies can undermine certain levels of scrutiny.

I'm calling Science out like it has never been called out.

I refer to 'brain' more often than mind. The mind cannot be biomechanically encoded in the brain. Some of it can. Canadian Wilder Penfield mapped out what is and isn't. The brain is attached to the mind in billions of ways. Each neuron is a little brain with multiple connections. The mind projects and lives beyond brain in ways this book will explore.

Physicist and mathematician of global renown, Edward Witten has said:

"I have a much easier time imagining how we understand the big bang, than I have imagining how we can understand consciousness," (Eben Alexander, Living in a Mindful Universe, p. 22).

Looking at the very something (the brain) that establishes the rules as to how we look at anything including ourselves, allows for true complexity. It's a game of mirrors, monuments and moments. Who we , are how we are and when we are is complex territory. When we aren't ourselves—who are we? When we are beside ourselves what does that entail? When a shooter's family says, so and so, wasn't himself that day—who was he?

Thoughts become an activity of perpetual discernment. In subtle ways, the 'who' you are, when you arrive at the end of this sentence, is a different who than the one starting the sentence. You are the only eye witness to it but really, you don't remember a thing. Everything happens incrementally.

THE WAGES OF SIN IS DEATH

Being lost in the funhouse, amusing ourselves to death, is great till we try to jump off the turntable and try to get our bearings.

Then everything changes. Fun just isn't fun anymore. Guys who are young and reckless eventually meet their match in various addictions, most commonly, alcohol. Often it is pain killers etc.

We are an addicted society, whether talking binge drinking or cell phone tyranny. We like to binge. Binge is our favourite mistake.

The initial excitement and inspiration for my book came from a scientific paper The Entropic Brain, referenced in Michael Pollan's book: HOW TO CHANGE YOUR MIND. Our next door neighbour, a librarian, says it's a popular book and it has done well for itself. Michael Pollan, a well-established writer, has launched himself into more dubious territory, documenting his drug experiences and suggesting what they reveal about our inner search for truth.

My next book will go into Pollan's book in detail. Suffice to say that Pollan agrees with Carl Jung who suggests people need a numinous experience to set the platform to help negotiate the second half of their lives. Having a mainstream writer willing to stick his head up and take a risk has encouraged me to come out of the closet in regards to my LSD experimentation.

The times we live in are unusual times. From Pollan's book, as I said, there was referenced a Science paper on *The Entropic Brain*. I dropped the book I was writing on metaphorical thought structures and dove into the topic: The Entropic Brain. It soon snowballed into this book you are now reading.

The Entropic Brain featured a spectrum approach to brain-mapping. I see an overarching spectrum as strategic to apprehending mental health and it is something I too have constructed, in my previous books. My spectrum, I call the Courtney Spectrum in my previous books, profiles degrees of inter-subjectivity and empathy. Low degrees of inter-subjectivity occur in Autistics, Asperger's etc. Simon Baron-Cohen has mapped out this end of the spectrum.

Close to this end of the spectrum (again Simon Baron-Cohen), is Male-Extreme Syndrome where male ideation has sacrificed emotional maturity for physical toughness. The tough male is blunted, de-emotionalized. It is rigorously upheld on sports teams, where emotions are ridiculed by locker-room mindsets. As the target of maleness is to not be a sissy, a pussy or crybaby, there is a lot of repression out of the gate in male developmental psychology. It's no wonder, with all this repression, males hold certain statistics. Mass murderers, domestic abusers, and the incarcerated are 90 percent male. Males certainly have their struggles with emotional disarray. They rarely have the wherewithal to put Humpty back together.

In Autism males outnumber females 5 to 1.

PIGGY

Hazing is an extreme form of perverse ideation that directly refutes 'caring' and implicates everyone involved and across social media. It's like *Lord of the Flies*. What hazing does is it destroys love.

The other end of 'my' spectrum, opposite low subjectivity, is profiled in Eric Kendal's book: *The Age of Insight*.

Insight, the Nobel prize-winner suggests, comes from empathy. Empathy is about walking a mile in the shoes of the 'other'. The doors of perception are cleansed in the act of reaching out. Synergy ignited by minds travelling into other minds erupted in the cafés of Vienna at the turn of the century. Like in Paris, painters, poets, philosophers created new concepts and new ways of understanding ourselves and the world. There was an explosion of interest in new and radical territory. People couldn't get enough of each other.

Empathy events reflect a mirroring process of self-into-self and other-into-self. Ideas were being harvested in Vienna and Paris and resultantly the world shifted on its axis . Relativity, Cubism, communication technologies, and so much more became quantum in positioning 'humans' in a new light, a new 'modern' light. By providing a new understanding of the human equation the equation itself was drastically altered.

The Entropic Brain has a slightly different spectrum than mine. For example we have different ideas on depression but *Entropic Brain* is a 'huge' paper with unrecognized ramifications. More than ever before we have to characterize the spectrum with appropriate language.

At first I didn't like the notion of Entropy. Entropy infers breakdown without possibility of reorganization or renewal.

Now I see entropy as a step in the perilous human journey: a way of losing ourselves to find ourselves. At the start, entropy for me was a negative term: the wind-up universe, winding down and falling apart. Initially I thought: ENTROPIC BRAIN – bad name, great discovery.

In ways that even the authors of that piece perhaps don't know it remains an insightful title and a powerful clue to what goes on in our brains when our minds shift gears. Particularly when our minds de-structure and lose compass. When north is no longer north and south no longer south we need to grapple.

It's those ways you are about to discover. This book, Neurogenesis, is also about Wolfgang Pauli and his portrait of Science as an ideation that has narrowed itself and by doing so sacrificed understanding. Pauli's case exemplifies a great deal about Science and how Science functions. Pauli was capable of confronting the psychologically and scientifically profound. Science wasn't.

"At the present time, a point has again been reached at which the rationalistic outlook has passed its zenith, and is found to be too narrow – too narrow to accept the existence of irrationalities which, if not understood, can find evil ways of expression," Wolfgang Pauli (David Lindorff, Pauli and Jung, p.196).

"There is a fundamental limitation on the knowledge obtainable at the atomic level, since, unlike in the macro world, any observation at the atomic level inevitably changes the state of a system under observation by interacting with it. Because every measurement creates a new set of conditions, the subatomic system must be treated as a whole," Wolfgang Pauli (David Lindorff, Pauli and Jung, p.198).

Art has fallen victim to the same organization of plasticity and mind structure as Science.It is inevitable. We as sociological creatures assume a socialized posture. All organizations (including churches and schools) become interpersonal organizations. Art, like Science, is an institutionalized event in the lives of citizenry. People have jobs and job descriptions. Unlike Science, Art was largely ignored as impractical, and compared to Science, an ignoble pursuit. Art was nothing to believe in. Like Santa Claus and the Stork one could and would abandon such fantasy with maturity. How wrong we were?

THE FIRST PERTURBATION: THANK GOD FOR FRANCE

When the Salon gallery selections became a rebellious issue in France, none other than Napoleon III put together the Salon des Refusés.

"From the works on show in the Salon des Refusés, educated observers, not least the artists themselves, could see that the jury was systematically barring from the Salon a particular style of painting in favour of the sort of art practised by many of its own members and taught at the École des Beaux Arts (p.91) …. Manet had no wish to enter the prestigious École des Beaux Arts, where originality and individuality were discouraged, and where students learned anatomy and geometry but not, bizarrely, how to paint," (The Judgment of Paris, p. 15).

Manet would head for a different learning environment where spontaneity and self-expression were stressed.

The painters refused by the traditional salon could hoist their works. With an infinite amount of wall space paintings came from far and wide, by buggy and by wheelbarrow. Canvasses, some ten feet tall threaded through the streets of Paris. Napoleon III personally attended the hanging of the exhibit in an attempt to get the better of this archetypal 'yellow vest-like' protest. The bottom line being: Art had run aground because the Establishment was increasingly out of touch with the creativity blossoming underfoot. There were issues of favouritism.

The Beaux-arts graduates had controlled the curation decisions as to who got their work shown. This was unfair enough but the problem went deeper. The Beaux arts group were a very conservative group—anti-imagination, anti-expression. They censored any imaginative leaps. Remember, there would be an avalanche of change once the scale and scope of Art itself changed. There would be a landslide. The roots of that change were in the Salon rebellion.

The traditionalists were sitting on a 'powder-keg' that was giving off sparks, and the future of Art and the blossoming of Impressionism, Fauvism, Expressionism, Surrealism, Dadaism etc. ...and everything that was spectacular in Art, was at stake. The Salon had doubters all along but no one had been able to take on the Art Establishment.

"Delacroix had once admitted in his journal, with pointed reference to Meissonier, that 'there is something else in painting besides exactitude and precise rendering from the model,'" (Ross King, The Judgment of Paris, p. 226).

We live in just such an age. Everything has to be rigidly and impeccably correct. It always comes back to this point where precision of detailing rules the roost and creative minds are excluded. Such detailing is optical and not consciousness-enabled. Everything is closed-shop as it was then. The schools of art cast a large shadow. The Art graduates have filled curation and exhibit manager roles and the mundane has ascended the power-ladder. It necessarily does when creativity plays no part and money calls the shots. Creativity by essence doesn't 'play' an institutional tune.

Like the actors of the silent screen who got tossed aside when talkies arrived, the big artists of our day will be chagrined tomorrow. Art today is all façade and no depth. It plays along with the crowd.

"The case of Meissonier is one that gives us pause to reflect about the variations of taste and the vicissitudes of glory. No painter was more adulated during his lifetime ... his reputation was global. But what remains today of this magnificence? Two decades later, Lionello Venturi's two-volume history of nineteenth-century French art, Modern Painters, made no mention of him whatsoever: Meissonier had vanished from the history of French art like a murdered enemy of Stalin airbrushed from an official Soviet photograph ... Rare is the artist on whom more prejudice – and even hatred – has accumulated than Meissonier. Not long ago the mere act of looking at one of his works was considered worthy of excommunication," (Ross King, The Judgment of Paris, p. 370-371).

It always comes to this, because as humans who fire and wire our brains into existence, we fall fatefully under the wheels of habit. Habit is an organizational imperative and antithetical to the creative act.

> **It is the humdrum and eternal yesterday,**
> **What always was and always comes anew,**
> **What holds good for tomorrow just because**
> **It held good for today. For man is made**
> **Of humdrum stuff and Habit is his nurse.**
> **(Schiller, in Pauli and Jung, p. 216).**

To sort ourselves out we need to investigate the psychologized, socialized mind. Everywhere we enable or disable consciousness. Needless to say it is easier to disable than enable. It's all about 'how' we believe.

> **Jesus loves me this I know**
> **for the bible tells me so.**
> **Little ones to him belong**
> **They are weak but he is strong**

If you sang this in Sunday school and you believed it, what does that mean? An act of believing entails certain things (neuroscience) and has certain ripple effects. In its ripple effects, regardless of whether the subject believed in, is even worthy of that belief, its psychological presence is real. Some of these bizarre cults like the yoga guy exist because people want to believe in Sadism and Masochism. It's dressed up as something else but that's it in a psychological nutshell. Belief is a state of mind. A child can't do all the analysis and diagnostics to accredit belief, but that's okay. Belief doesn't rely on proof. It is an exercise of faith. A child takes a lot of things on faith. Faith in the social structure, school, church, parents. So it's not that unusual.

If belief gave you comfort in rough times and improved your psychological outlook, is it untrue or unreal? If it gives you a stronger heart, and better blood pressure and a reason to get up in the morning, then what's the deal?

The effect is felt and the belief acts conceptually to frame an interface between child and belief. If the belief is a shelter in the time of storm, that's good.

If you develop over time a close relationship with Jesus and certain events seem to reinforce your belief then Jesus is stabilizing your reality. Why would you throw Jesus under the bus with Superman and the Green Hornet, and the Bobbsey Twins-- if your psyche was improved by the belief? If Jesus steers you through a deep depression or some traumatic incident, how 'real' is that?

If someone comes along and says Jesus isn't real, he's just a psychological crutch, training wheels for beginners, should you see their view as more objective? That is the question. It is true that innocence is treasured precisely because a capacity for belief has not yet been irrevocably damaged. This is why Holden Caulfield had a mission.

Much that is wrong with Art and Science has to do with 'thinking' itself. Art graduates get schooled in an education system that is mapped out and prescriptively 'known'. You 'think' your way through with whatever thinking system is in vogue given one's instructors and course-calendar preferences. A capacity to innocently respond to a piece that might offer up 'newness' is quickly mired in the accepted judgemental alignment, the milieu, of the academic 'take'. This is 'set' within the collective plasticity, the bureaucratic alignment, and the very language and level of discourse. And it culminates in who is allocated wall space. In the end the choice relies on flimsy ill-warranted criteria, and complete presumption within the establishment.

At a local gallery, I used to buy the latest issue of Arabella magazine, encouraged by its voluptuous format and orgasmic presentation of colour. I soon realized this is a magazine and an art world not wanting to confront in any way, shape or form, the highly charged psychological age we live in. They would sooner pretend that status quo will prevail and that human beings will have walls to hang their collections on. The role of Art is to get us away from the shadows on the wall.

After all this 'collectability' is speculation rarely a causality of future interpretation. Like in Meissonier's case it depends on the world staying as boring as it is. Taste is a precognitive assumption. It is a presupposition that gets more radically diffused daily into acceptance motifs. Such assumptions by-pass the necessary aspect of art—the untidy creative act.

Most in the Art world grow thick skins and lose the ability to feel-see. A mind cut loose from its feelings is a piece of information, without a heartbeat.

If you are good looking and paint the same shit as everyone else you'll grace the walls and pages of the Art world. All you have to agree to is implicit and never stated. You can't say your inspiration is cash even though it is. The send up of Art in the novel, *The Italian Teacher*, encapsulates the popular view of the Art world. Art is flimsy and flaky.

"Marsden wants to go to *Sensation*, an edgy show at the Royal Academy featuring contemporary British art, among which a frozen head made from the artist's blood, a dead shark mounted behind glass, and child mannequins with mouths like anuses and noses like penises …. Marsden stands on the other side of the glass tank, appraising the pickled shark. Peeping into open jaw, he says, 'Is this good, enduring work, Charles? Or is it taxidermy?" (Tom Rachman, The Italian Teacher, p. 229).

Outrage is not what Art is about. The newspapers are full of outrage. Art is about breaking on through to the other side. Artists are portrayed as not capable of saying anything intelligible. Artists are kept on a tight leash by managers in case they say something stupid beyond stupid and thereby blow the whole charade.

LET US COMPARE MYTHOLOGIES

Perception itself is a crutch any way we look at it. You want to perceive the world you perceive. Any way of looking at something involves capacity for perception and awareness. How much capacity depends on the individual. Perception also contains its own arc or field of reference, its own thought architecture. Our vistas are created by who we are, by biases entrenched and attitudes embedded. We hardly ever think about how we think and why we think the way we do. We never ask ourselves: Do I need to change the way I think to avoid mental illness?

Men have looped brains. It is their undoing. By scoring lower on Empathy they sacrifice important conceptuality. They drill down, they unpackage, but beyond that things get murky. Yesterday a study said women's brains are on average 3 years younger than male counterparts.

The male ego prevents a range of sympathy and empathy completely necessary for emotional maturity. A lot of this is tied in with athletics and the male orientation protocol.

Males have a male code. That code is anti-feeling and anti-intellectual. You can't have feelings and you can't talk about feelings without straying from the male code. Holden Caulfield's roommate Stradlater embodied maleness. He was unscrupulous according to Holden.

"It wasn't allowed for students to borrow faculty guys' cars, but all the athletic bastards stuck together. In every school I've gone to, all the athletic bastards stick together," (J.D. Salinger, Catcher in the Rye, p. 43).

Ultimately we believe 'in' how we fire and wire our interface with reality. When we stop believing that we are in deep doo doo. We are dissociated. Dissociation can triumph over coherence. When things don't add up and when things don't make sense the shit hits the fan.

When it does? Look out! Duck and cover!

Without coherence the world fragments. It dislocates itself with semi-arbitrariness. You can't bet on anything. You can't depend on anything.

However efficient or deficient is our thinking, so too our future. If deficient, we pay the piper. We become mentally congestive, entangled in the mindless day-to-day. By having a better psychological outlook we will fare better and enjoy life more. There have been innumerable giants in the land of thinking, mostly male because that's what society allowed and endorsed at the time. Thinking is no longer thought about. It is taken for granted. It is completed before it happens.

People didn't always think about thinking. Yet arguably all Greek drama is about thinking, about actions and consequences. By the time Oedipus hits the road for Colonus, with his blindness and his cane, he is a broken but enlightened man. Shakespeare is full of stuff about thinking. Falstaff''s thinking diverges from Prince Hal's. Hamlet's thinking is everything to him the most important reality. Thinking is the method in Hamlet's madness.

KEPLER: THE INTERNAL AND EXTERNAL

When you read the following quotation by Johan Kepler written a few hundred years ago, when there were no text books to stand on, no shoulders of giants to peer from, it is easy to see what impressed Nobel Physicist Wolfgang Pauli. Kepler was describing his own mind in action. Pauli was 'into' how the mind works.

What we have is Kepler breaking down how all minds work. Making conclusions from the externally perceived and lining these up with internal ideas 'awakens' connections. Many of these connections build speculation upon speculation. The things in the outside world can't help but continuously remind us of what we know. It's hard to disentangle speculations from our ways of knowing what is known.

The soul for Kepler was a place hidden from view. There are things hidden in the soul that can shine forth revealing potentiality without us knowing whence they came. You cannot arrive at such territory through **discursive reasoning**. Normal cognition is discursive. It hinges directly on what is known.

Scientific reasoning is discursive and cognitive, and incorporates the 'building blocks' of a type of understanding. The known way of knowing things prevails unwaveringly and automatically. The other thinking is more imagining and less structural, less 'cog' like... something more akin to something we allow to happen because of natural human instincts. The thinking here happens because you are open to its happening. This means not being clogged with normalization.

"For to know is to compare that which is externally perceived with inner ideas and to judge that it agrees with them, a process which Proclus expressed very beautifully by the word 'awakening' as from sleep. For, as the perceptible things which appear in the outside world make us remember what we knew before, so do sensory experiences, when consciously realized; call forth intellectual notions that were already present inwardly; so that which formally was hidden in the soul, as under the veil of potentiality, now shines therein in actuality. How, then, did they (intellectual notions) find

ingress? I answer: all ideas or formal concepts of the harmonies...lie in those beings that possess the faculty of rational cognition, and they are not at all received within by discursive reasoning; rather they are derived from a natural instinct and are inborn in those beings as a number (an intellectual thing) of petals in a flower," Johan Kepler, as quoted, (David Lindorff, Pauli and Jung, p. 86-87).

Awakening

The blossom is inside you. It's natural. Certainly Blake and Picasso would suggest children potentiate creativity naturally. Again and again the language will confuse. Rationalism is a sub-category of mind. Creativity is a sub-category. They often work in an interfused manner but suffer most frequently when rationality assumes a presumptive 'master role'. The book, *The Master and the Emissary*, by Iain McGilchrist is beyond recommendable, it is genius. The left brain wants to package you and fill in the blanks with you, regardless of your 'deepest' wishes. The left brain wants to expedite you.

"The left hemisphere's 'stickiness', its tendency to recue to what it is familiar with, tends to reinforce whatever it is already doing. There is a reflexivity to the process, as if trapped in a hall of

mirrors: it only discovers more of what it already knows, and it only does more of what it is already doing. The right hemisphere by contrast, seeing more of the picture, and taking a broader perspective," (McGilchrist, The Master and the Emissary, p. 86).

If you want to know about left brain and right brain: read McGilchrist.

Does your consciousness work for you? Are you trapped day in and day out in a hall of mirrors?

Many people these days are feeling the bite. They want to move from an unstable psychic condition to a stable psychic condition. They want to be at ease, at ease in their own skin, in their own life.

Many people on medication, and I was one, feel metabolically out of step with their own central nervous system. During my 'back' episode I felt jerked around by slow and fast acting morphine.

How does consciousness work and how does it implicate your psyche?

Why does it work the way it does? Are there alternative ways it works for you, in different phases of your life?

These are of course fundamental questions about our existence. Arguably, a failure to negotiate the learning curve in this area, of reconciling ourselves to ourselves, could have fateful results. Indeed those results, POSITIVE OR NEGATIVE OUTCOMES, are registered in the human condition as manifestations of our mental health or lack thereof.

Is consciousness fun for you? It's an important question as it determines your get-up-and-go. If your get-up-and-go has got-up-and-gone, you need to introduce new thresholds. Playfulness on your own terms is important. It's not about pay-to-play culture.

If consciousness is pained and not fun, you'll learn to shy away from consciousness. You will settle for keeping things unconscious. People meandering through life in a subcritical mode are the norm. They sweep life's consternation under the carpet. They repress their voice and their true identity. They fit in.

THE ENTROPIC BRAIN

Subcritical and critical awareness are differentiated in a way that makes sense. The first, subcritical, is 'every-day' as we get lulled by the momentum of existence. The second being critical, can make you feel that in the moment, your whole life might explode. There is a crisis of self-identification. It becomes important, to be present, as you put your life on the line to individuate who you are.

The first can make you believe nothing is going wrong, and the second that life is falling apart. The depth of self-examination and self-scrutiny is important.

Normalization is the process of typical reasoning, something constantly shored up by bias. We pay to play. Every step we take, from our first to our last, is incorporated within this normalization structure. We accept without reserve the future as it comes to us by the Media-messengers who deliver it hot and cold, good cop bad cop...and we take it in. It is goop.

Some of the root causes exist within the inherited paradigm of what Science is and what it isn't.

Like everything else the dust settles on human culture and to change any methodology midstream causes uproar and fisticuffs between the old and the new. Change is threatening, Change necessarily causes deep rooted anxiety and animosity and people rally to protect their turf. A 'fight-or-flight' response is elemental. It is primitive. It is pre-culture. It is often necessary.

"It is also proposed that entry into primary states depends on a collapse of the normally highly organised activity within the default-mode network (DMN) and a decoupling between the DMN and the medial temporal lobes (which are normally significantly coupled)," (The Entropic Brain, p. 9).

Highly organized activity within the range of acceptable Normalization graduates to our undoing. Fight or flight makes you take notice. *The Entropic Brain* presents a theory of conscious states informed by neuroimaging research with psychedelic drugs. Psychedelic drugs can plunge us into experiential territory where the cultural 'self' disappears. This can be terrifying. It's also terrifying in real life with depression, or dementia or bi-polarity. Dislocation is also often the reality of pulling up roots in a relationship or job. You literally change your location. Dislocation, dissociation or de-structuring are used to describe a reality diverging quickly from what it has been. One can set the stage with a psychedelic experience.

The problem for Science is the same as the problem with Art. <u>It has to do with the brain's security policy. We become creatures of habit because we fire and wire the same self every day. The brain becomes layered.</u>

Like a grain in a slab of wood, life leaves its mark and its contours on our brain. We expect, first and foremost, to daily discover a world outside ourselves that from Kindergarten on can be assimilated with reasonable effort.

Nobody else gets too excited so you learn to subdue excitement. School yard threats or direct confrontations get assimilated as rites of passage.

Psychedelic experience can show us that a lot of what we pre-ordained as such and such is actually not written in stone, is actually up for grabs. Indeed the whole rites to passage is contrived and differs tribe to tribe. This comes back to the argument between what is soft-wired and what is hard-wired. Sometimes things ingrained by normalization are so emphatic as to seem hard-wired. The bottom line; criticality can be a good thing if you want a cascade of change to transform you. The self we contrived was one schooled in wanting to measure up to implanted expectations. In measuring up we can lose sight of who we are.

FOUNTAIN OF YOUTH

Ponce De Leon, I believe it was, went searching for the Fountain of Youth. These explorers and discoverers fascinated me. The imagination ran wild with new shores to see. Have you ever asked yourself--What would the Fountain of Youth look like? How would you recognize it?

The Fountain of Youth, if it exists, is within our mind's own features and is something known as NEUROGENESIS.

Neurogenesis is the birth of the new. Neurogenesis is the birth of new neurons. Neuroplasticity can change you by migrating firing and wiring patterns across the hundred billion neuron universe. Neuroplasticity allows you to stake out new territory in yourself—in your 100 billion neuron, 3 pound universe you can fire and wire new habits.

Neurogenesis isn't part of the finite brain at all. We are talking brand spanking new neurons and hence new neurology. Why do we have a potential for new neurons when the hundred billion neuron universe is more than we can handle?

That's a good question. Neurogenesis can birth neurons dedicated to and excited by new tasks; creative tasks that percolate within each of us, addressing the need for novelty, change and meaning. The pursuit of meaning is natural for an evolving brain. By bringing new ideas into our make-up we source new-mind, new-brain, new-body territory. It is a fountain of youth. If we access it better than we currently can it might allow us to grow a new spine, a new arm.

Of course old ideas die hard. People still look for the fountain of youth, in Botox, in plastic surgery, in nutrition, or creams or exercise. Most would like to find it in a pill.

Brain plasticity can change the self. Lots of people have faced off with a disease and found strength they never knew they had. Epiphany can re-characterize a person and infuse them with new life. Neuroplasticity and Neurogenesis keeps healing possible.

Delusion and self-deception, denial and going along with the crowd, are the cornerstones taken for granted in the individual's cultural modus operandi.

Tons of literature flushes out the more meaningful thought trajectories but there is diminishing effort across the population to think about thinking. Nobody has time to think about what they are doing anymore. All these time-saving devices take up all our time. Like sheep we run fast to the slaughter.

It is not the wisdom of ancient self-realization and evolution that informs us today. The digital revolution has rendered much of that unreachable. Much of the knowledge of the ancients has been compromised. Cars are smart. TVs are smart, phones are smart---but people? - not so much.

Science has ignored much of the learning that goes on beyond its modus operandi, the sort symbolized by a graduated cylinder or a Bunsen burner. The scientific definition resides most firmly in the nature of measurement and the stock tools of the trade.

Arguably the world is moving so fast that both Science and Art are being left behind like any other rusty anachronism.

The future is a gateway drug to more of the same.

More detachment and more dissociation are on the horizon. Like the Animals of Animal Farm we are being boondoggled. .

You'll never have your wits about you if you don't exercise discretion. Life comes at us so fast one moment displaces another. We crave this speed of change. It fuels our attention span even as it shortens it. Information trends change. We jockey for position.

It's this that falsifies the brain incrementally and unnoticeably over time. People become entrenched and embedded in an oxygenation process, in a posture and in a metabolism. Stress is routine. Posture and breathing absorb that. Thoughts are the same every day. The psyche absorbs that. The body keeps score and the mind keeps score and you keep running up the tab.

We rise and fall with the occasion, all circumstantial. We go through a digital turnstile without really ever arriving anywhere. We are constantly white knuckling and white-water rafting the TV screen while sublimating our energy. The shoreline flies by. Nothing registers but the speed. In the end nothing defines us but the speed of interference with our thinking. If the speed stops we are instantly bored.

Even the rituals are point-counterpoint so Christmas comes and goes and the other holidays follow suit. Nothing registers. Our moods are regulated by occasion realities. We pull our thinking up short at weddings or funerals. We pass through a travelogue of rooms, each room demanding something different not something more. Consent is manufactured. We run with the crowd. We all fall down.

THE SUBJECT OF SCIENCE

Science goes about its work with its eye on certain things looking for ways to demonstrate reliability, focusing perennially on the measurement of properties of things. The tangible causal world is the world on our doorsteps but its visibility and viability are no longer established, as Pauli pointed out.

In Physics everything today is at a standstill, nothing is happening. Scientists are grabbing for straws. And strings. We got to the end of the narrative that featured breakthrough after breakthrough. Now we're in a different chapter.

Each mind construct admits to itself a continuous stream of biases based on knowledge. We presume too much in the case of Science. We think Science cleans up superstition with clarity and certainty. By ignoring the Scientist's psyche, Science has confused realms of understanding. They have applied what they know to what is unknown, thinking it more of the same.

The Radical truth is: Science has led us to the threshold of uncertainty, where we come up short with our measuring instruments and our know-how. It's not the fault of Science that we can't scale reality to fit into our telescopes and test tubes. It's just the way it is.

It is Science's fault that they rarely acknowledge all the holes in the big picture. It's Science's fault that they shy away from the sources that induce imagination. Science is slow on the uptake of how involved our brains are and need to be in any revelations forthcoming. The trajectory of any thought and knowledge sequences, stemming from the old paradigms, is retarded by the gravitational pull of the paradigm.

Implicating constantly traditional subservience to fact not fancy, Science censors knowledge by defining what knowledge is and more importantly presuming on what it isn't. This debilitates any thoughtful investigation and more important and to the point, any imaginative event horizon. The imagination is truncated back through what-is fact. Like a hot air balloon on a tether it is tethered to a way of doing. Science has lost itself in its own self-congratulatory insidiousness. It eats its own tail, dissects its own stomach all the while placidly circumventing the brain from seeing itself.

Even neuroscience falls prey to the same delivery service, to the same thought structures. Much research is wasted because parameters are imposed that hinge on fundable ideas which are necessarily ideas already understood.

Take ART

The prescripts in the art world are all, because of bureaucratic necessity, left brain and inherently academic, which is to say based on knowledge. Those 'connected' in the art world are fraudulent conspirators always pumping the tires, never kicking them. At best, art is a fragile hot house sort, of consciousness mustered by the elite.

Nobody knows shit about ART anymore. The trivial and the trite contest favourably against the profound, as if birds of a feather.

TRACEY

In a museum in Amsterdam (January 2003) there was a Tracey Emin exhibit we went to see. In an adjacent room on display were five large things. Were they bears in wax?

What could this possibly be? We approached stealthfully. Was it alive? It looked fresh.

On closer look …. here ladies and gentlemen we have five turds (juicy) each 3 to 5 feet long by 18 inches or more thick, in some kind of glaze. Like I said, it looked fresh, fresh as a daisy.

As a comment on Art this is a great piece. Rarely, especially in the Art world, is there such self-disclosure.

This is Art today in many places. Shit glazed over and mounted. The rest is spin doctrine.

Art courses are categorical and informational. All this is inherently different in its constructs and its follow-through. Subsequently-defined reality makes everything derivative and discursive. A vision too far from anything born of the instigated imagination involving originality. The art industry and networks of Art school graduates are all fabricating what their subject matter is in an effort to consolidate some sense of market value. They pretend they have their fingers on the creative pulse. Nothing could be further from the truth.

Without market value assessment efficiency, they don't have jobs.

THIRD EYE

Artistry has lost in this process its Third Eye alliance with a host of more ambiguous relevancies than dollars and cents. The third eye cannot spring from information sessions and course calendar allocation. It is necessarily contrasted and differentiated from unabashed creativity. For one thing there is nothing unabashed about it. Like Science the new art is a paradigm-crippled, cognitive derivative, pre-packaged and pre-digested product. Each moment inherits from the previous moment the conditions of being, and with it, the packaging.

"The interchangeability of art and money – the completeness of their correlation – suggests that there is something rotten about both. This has nothing to do with whether art is good and money is bad, but with the fact that they belong to radically different realms. Or at least they did until Warhol confused them by forcing them together. Giving each the value of the other he devalued both …. What looks like a dialectic is not really one. Art and money do not share common existential ground; they have no essential connection," (Donald Kuspit, The End of Art, p. 149).

There is no existential essential reality to Art today. Once vision, which is what Art is about, is lost in the collective unconscious, Art is lost. Art is irredeemable. Art is anybody's game, anybody's hustle. Exit through the gift shop. There will always be paintings on the wall—what's the diff?

The pretense within the art community is aggressively formatted because of the lip service to things creative. The artsy establishment gets real defensive, real quick, when you think art has an existential or social role to play.

Bring on the clowns.

Art galleries are raiding art graduate schools for new art. There is no new art. There is only derivative art. The imagination has dried up. It has no neurological basis for existence. It's an Art House built on the sand cut off from the necessary and nourish-able root systems.

The professionals lose the 'eye' from looking at the assembly line of 'things'. You fire and wire the wrong loops. You become habituated in discernment faculties. You go blind.

Eventually Art settles into axioms and expectations built on knowledge.

When it comes to creativity, ART is out of the picture. Art as academic subject matter is inherently ignorant because the way the brain fires and wires 'normally' is antithetical to creative apprehension. Jumping through the hoops of the system lands you a paper on the wall; it won't make you creative.

New art trends, chosen with the analytical, academic, and imagination-deficient minds fail to resolve what humans need from art. What we need from art is a big picture of what we are up to. The cost to put a painting on the wall inhibits, then prohibits, real art.

Because of firing and wiring habits and dysfunctional criteria traditionalized and waxed over, there is no discerning voice. The grant system substantiates entitlement and hierarchy, entirely independent of merit. Beyond this these High Priests of Art muddy the waters young artists drown in. They do it with their ensconced triteness. Youth should have an outlet in Art.

David Hockey is a decent man.

But he ain't Picasso.

He's an attendant lord, one that will do to swell a progress, to quote Eliot. The very fact that the Art world is ass-backwards dictates the sort of painter called upon to fill the role of heir apparent to Picasso. He has to be safe.

Everything in art is based on who knows who and who has the blessing of this or that curator.

It's a façade held up to the light of day by mental midgets who don't dare take their own read, for fear of stepping on the toes of the Greek Chorus.

Art has lost its authenticity, its soul and its moorings. It is a manufactured taste to facilitate a pre-digested, pre-surveyed reality. People feel powerless and ignorant if they can't spot the next great one so they improvise. Curators are illusionists following the path of least resistance which is always the one that makes business sense. David Hockney isn't going to turn anyone's brain upside down. He certainly won't hang a grand piano from a tree or phone for a pizza, with a lobster.

Someday owning a David Hockney may be akin to admitting your deficiency. Like Meissonier who was run out of the Louvre when the winds of valuation took a 180.

Certainly, many of the so-called collectable artists will flounder.

The important thing with Art is getting it. Peggy Guggenheim got it. This is why so many are frozen in fear in galleries. They can't find a voice to describe what they like or don't like. How did Peggy Guggenheim look at the far out the outrageous and recognize Art?

What if they made a mistake? What if their ignorance IS EXPOSED?

That's the point of Art—to expose our ignorance.

What if they don't get the joke? Peggy Guggenheim was ridiculed but in a twist of irony her collection is worth billions.

After Napoleon III gave the outsiders their first boost, the tide would turn. In a few short decades the Art world would not only see the likes of

>Monet and Manet,

>they would see Van Gogh's self-portraits,

>Picasso and Braque and Duchamp's Cubism, Magritte and Dali's

>mind-blowing dreamscapes.

>Freud would happen and Jung. And a patent clerk named Einstein

>would set sail.

Art has always been a flagship for civilization. As reflected in cave paintings, earlier exhibitors of art wanted to connect. Connection fosters civilization.

Meissonier was authentic to the last detail. Napoleon's armour, the horse, the uniform, was all exactingly well-researched. Meissonier was perfect. Perfection can be sterile.

He was found out.

In the early 1880's Vincent Van Gogh wrote, "Painting is a faith," he declared. It is "not created by hands alone, but by something that wells up from a deeper source in our souls …. with regard to adroitness and technical skills in art I see something that reminds me of what in religion may be called self-righteousness," (Donald Kuspit, End of Art, p. 143).

Vincent identified with the "…outcasts and felt the artist in general was an outcast – which made Christ the most outcast of all artists – but he felt that art could redeem their lives and show their humanity, just as he felt being an artist could redeem his life and allow him to show his humanity …. Van Gogh wanted to show the humanity of art, which saved it from self-righteousness, from a hollow pride of craft and the arrogance of self-sufficiency," (Donald Kuspit, The End of Art, p. 144).

"Van Gogh deeply identified with Christ the artist, fusing his identity with Christ's, to the extent of attacking 'the Pharisees of art' the way Christ attacked the Pharisees who academicized religion, turning it into authoritarian dogma and

lifeless ritual …. His art preached universal empathy rather than blind obedience to aesthetic law. It was informed by the spirt not the letter of religion; painting was a spontaneous sermon rather than a theological lesson in correct religious thinking," (Donald Kuspit, The End of Art, p. 145).

Art is necessary in many ways to fulfill the transcendence motifs associated with religion.

Art has academicized creativity and originality.

The local art group has a new phrase: community and creativity.

This is bunk.

They are closed shop, the dying aftermath of a hand-me-down world of colonialist stylized attitudes. The dogma is intercellular. Art was often associated with hierarchy and culture. Before Caravaggio only important people were painted. The privileged still see in the exercise of privilege an inherent leg-up in taste and valuation. That Art exists as a 'cult' of conservatism is old hat. It is the perennial and inescapable fact of brain plasticity that to be creative you have to fire and wire creativity. Local artists are simply tactical strategists. They are self-righteous and contemptuous because sterility breeds contempt.

Bureaucracy aims to subdue unrest. What better way than to have those in control of art reduce it to ineffectiveness. Art can't be discovered in a university course calendar. Art can't be engendered in the minds and hearts of the aloof child decked out in privilege. Privilege prevents consciousness. How many Art graduates actually practice Art... if we look at the last 50 years? For most Art is and was a dead end. The lucky others emerge as parasites in the system.

White people can be blamed in a fashion, in that certain power-mongering Whites have succumbed to the artificial and the decorous, the 'symbols' of colonial privilege.

Other peoples' truths are melted down into cold cash purchases. Indigenous Tribes with more profound imaginations have been wiped out. The embroidery and the piano lessons fall short of the quest. The everyday white person pays the price. At restaurants I see brokenness all around. Families are broken. Many white people live in poverty and anguish. It's the other white people, the ones in charge, who perpetuate a mythology of over-arching intelligence masking profound ignorance. It's the wealthy whites who don't give a shit, who pose the problem.

WHAT IS NOBILITY?

In Vienna in 1900 there were thousands manufacturing pianos, so the nobility could distinguish itself as higher creatures. Fine arts belonged to refined people. Fine arts could further evolution. Shouldn't it?

This would be challenged soon enough. Money buys privilege and privilege buys art. This bastardizes art. Art loses its psychological need to exist. It becomes a subcategory of a larger Normalization.

Breton saw the degeneration of what Art was about and what needed to be apparent in Art.

"Dream must be mingled with action ... The true power, lyrical and efficacious, should result from a communication with one with the other …. The linking of the time and space of the dream to those of the world about us; then, his illustrations, from his own experience, of the quite remarkable workings of le *hasard objectif*, or objective chance, as the visible and always surprising link of one world to the other, by chance and by some sort of interior necessity. With this is intertwined a sort of disquisition on the place of love in the universe, the revolutionary character of antibourgeois feeling as it takes on and conquers the platitudes of bourgeois existence," (André Breton, Communicating Vessels, p. xiii).

We are trapped in the platitudes of bourgeois existence. Breton and Duchamp lost sleep because they could see the bourgeois manufacturing of a taste completely in accord with lowest common denominator apprehension of inspiration and creation. What Breton and Duchamp feared happening has happened. The bourgeois have dictated what Art is. The superficial society tyrannizes us with their taste and Art bows down to cash.

Vincent Van Gogh railed against bourgeois self-righteousness in his uncle's prestigious Paris gallery which got him no pats on the back, no employee of the month awards. His uncle hastily transferred the vociferous Vincent to London. The very nature of the human brain and human perception is to reside in a circumvented reality. The shoppers wanted comfortable art then and they didn't want to be told anything different, not even by Vincent Van Gogh.

THIS IS IT, what humans are in every moment up against. Within our self-deception we author our own destruction by choosing our own level of distraction. That's why real Art stood up against the status quo and a consumer-defined market. Impressionism, Cubism, Surrealism, Dadaism, etc. tried to shake up our illusions about who and how we are people. Francis Bacon disclaimed his contemporaries, harking back to Picasso, when asked to designate someone who was inspiring.

Warhol made art American. He sucked the life out of it and glammed it.

He made art quirky and stupid. **"One needs a specific image to unlock the deeper sensations, and the mystery of accident and intuition to create the particular ... Pop art is made for kicks. Great art gives kicks too, but it also unlocks the valves of intuition and perception about the human situation at a deeper level,"** (Francis Bacon: A Retrospective Exhibition p. 42).

As creatures of habit we solidify ourselves in our roles. Art, Science and everything becomes part of the commonplace. We successfully reduce ourselves to the packaging and scheduling of daily activities. The prison is real in the most constitutional sense. It's in our blood, how we think and perceive. We need Art to save us from ourselves. But Art has gone AWOL.

SYNAPSE AND SELF

Axons are the brain's mind becoming manifest. They form physical networks that become the brain. Myelin coating ensures that these neural routes are established in fact, rooted in biochemistry and held in place by biomagnetism. If you are going to change your mind you have to upset the biochemical and magnetic reality of physical fact. Trying to uproot and rid oneself of certain memories can be painful. Like ripping up the tracks in and out of grand central station our myelin coated axons are like pipelines in the earth and they hold the mind in their grip.

Fire and wire potentiation and patterning depends on resonance. One becomes aligned with change or ensconced in habit. The easiest approach is by way of the imagination free of the normalized subcritical lapsed mindscapes. Magical thinking is something we discover within ourselves. Magical thinking is like dancing. It doesn't get bunched up in verbs and nouns. It doesn't have to make sense.

"Magical thinking is a style of cognition in which supernatural interpretations of phenomena are made. Magical thinking is more likely in situations of high uncertainty because there is a greater opportunity for dreaming up explanations that lack an evidence base (Friston, 2010) …. The popularity of magical thinking also suggests that there is some enjoyment in uncertainty, perhaps because it promotes imaginative and creative thinking – and that this is associated with positive affect," (The Entropic Brain: a theory of conscious states informed by neuroimaging research with psychedelic drugs).

Art thresholding with uncertainty maximizes possibility and potentiation. **This can be immediate feedback of a positive feeling, a positive electrical surge. Uncertainty promotes imaginative and creative thinking.**

Entropy Always

If you are breaking off a relationship or taking a psychedelic drug it can blow your mind. When your mind is blown the structures of your thinking disappear. Often you are left alone in a big ocean with a single piece of driftwood keeping you afloat the world looks suddenly different.

Dissociation can seem absolute. You might feel you are living a lie and hence constantly in deep conflict with yourself. This can be emotionally exhausting- birth and death co-activated in a fight to the finish.

The self can feel lost, even extracted from reality, because the common business-as-usual patterns of firing and wiring aren't operative. The mind is rattling around in the brain wondering what the next step is. It's in this 'zero' moment where all prescriptiveness fails that anything can happen. When life is up for grabs it leaves behind the gravity of assurance.

You don't need drugs to have a disconcerting or de-composing event. Any dissociation, any mental illness can plunge us into uncertainty which is why psychedelic drugs help us understand the mind.

"It does not seem to be an exaggeration to say that psychedelics, used responsibly and with proper caution, would be for psychiatry what the microscope is for biology and medicine or the telescope is for astronomy. These tools make it

possible to study important processes that under normal circumstances are not available for direct observation (Grof, 1980)," (The Entropic Brain: a theory of conscious states informed by neuroimaging research with psychedelic drugs, p. 3).

All change involves the death of the old: the birth of the new. In the case of a psychedelic drug we can be dealing with a revealed self. There is a Kundalini effect when our psyche doubles back on us. This for some (most) can be horrifying as they try to hang on to their preferred and historically established version of the truth. Blow your mind was the battle cry of the sixties and for good reason. Your old habits and moorings could in a flash seem a heap of broken images.

Going through hell for a heavenly cause is what entropy can bring about. Caught in the Venturi effect of the falling debris of self-hood, one gets a glimpse of a whole new self. It's similar in a creative effort with Art as one presses the edges of self, against uncertainty, thereby discovering a voice.

This is why Pauli was attracted to dreamscape analysis. He wanted to complete the cycle of understandings in a Jungian sense. Going through hell for a heavenly cause is the archetypal perilous journey. It's not risk for a physical 'rush' like a snowboarder projecting the gyrating body through space. It's the leap of faith inside the self, over the abyss of the psychically undifferentiated collective unconscious. Over the anonymity of the human chorus.

The journey for the psyche is always evolving into higher platforms of complexity, different areas of motivation. Most Scientists and most human beings prefer to bury their heads in the daily din. Like ostriches they prefer to defer the threat, mediate it through normalization, and hope that Nineveh doesn't come calling. Jonah was called out by God, swallowed by a whale and coughed up a new man.

The whale is a metaphor for a complex thing, a larger than life monster that swallowed Jonah and could swallow us. The whale is a whale of a metaphor, a metaphor's metaphor.

When the whale coughed Jonah up he was born again. He was ready to measure up to a calling, to be born again..

An arousing inciting stimulus is what the best art is about.

I CHING

"Pauli drew another parallel from the hexagram *chen* (thunder) in the *I-Ching* ('the arousing, inciting movement'), which he interpreted as describing such a moment: chen is symbolized by thunder which bursts forth from the earth and by its shock causes fear and trembling ... the fear and trembling engendered by shock come to an

individual at first in such a way that he sees himself placed at a disadvantage as against others. But this is only transitory. When the ordeal is over, he experiences relief, and thus the very terror he had to endure at the outset brings good fortune in the long run," (David Lindorff, Pauli and Jung, p. 102).

Transitory hell can sometimes be what life is about. It can be what a psychedelic trip can be about. But when it is over the emergent identity feels the experience one of good fortune.

Entropy, though transitory, is an all-in, or all-out thing. The artist is the Shaman leading the people out of the wilderness towards self-knowing. For the real artist it is heart and soul the singularly most important motif that voice and vision surface. This entails frequent emotional dislocation, and is consequently painful and extreme. This doesn't mean you leave your wife and 5 kids behind like Gaugin, and run away from contextual responsibility. The trick is in the mind.

To dislocate a whole society, as currently necessary, is to dislocate the locked-in syndrome of rote-styled bias. It is the same with the self. To accomplish this with the self is self-realization.

Each painting is a Rorschach whether you like it or not. You meet a painting in the middle. Much of what you see in today's Art is preordained, by what Art has become. There are no entry points. There is no middle. Today's art is all surface gesture. If you try to see-feel today's Art you get deflected. Art is creativity and creativity is an existential process not a monetary discipline. **Art is not a business course at Harvard.**

I'm with Francis Bacon in respecting chance.

"What I do believe is that chance and accident are the most fertile things at any artist's disposal at the present time," (Francis Bacon: A Retrospective Exhibition p. 47).

The fertility of CHANCE is the garden of the universe. One sets sail without destination.

And when you look at Art you have to come to a piece fresh; in spite of, and even if you know the painter's work. There is a high degree of entropy in creativity and you have to hand over your criteria-obsessed shopping list to discover the where and the how of the 'dislocation'.

"Art should be something which reverberates within your psyche, it disturbs the whole life cycle within a person. It affects the atmosphere

in which you live. Most of what is called art, your eye just flows over. It may be charming or nice, but it doesn't change you," (Francis Bacon: A Retrospective Exhibition, p. 48).

To re-acclimatize the mind is the reality of Art. Divergence, dislocation and dissociation are part of the opportunity of plasticity. Beating oneself up existentially is fashionable and a necessary part of the journey. The significance of voice is in its arrival after a sojourn of non-existence.

Lately my wife has been second guessing herself on the one hand and the next minute throwing herself under the bus. Our attention span for self-scrutiny is the most important feature of consciousness navigation. Self-questioning is good for the soul.

One backs up from imposing an idea about reality on reality. One takes a good hard look at the self. And one paints their way out of a corner. The corner is a mental architecture of status quo where you have been pre-positioned by the shaping factors in your life.

If you want to evaluate yourself accurately you hypothesize earnestly and contritely, knowing what is at stake. Life is an experiment. You are the guinea pig. What is at stake is saving the self, saving mental health, saving the soul. What is at stake is the perilous and often painful journey of self-realization.

There is no victory lap just some occasional moments, a sense of confirmation and existential liberty. (Or as Leonard would say, a broken and a lonely Hallelujah.)

What is at stake in a neuroscientific sense is still Salvation. A rose by any other name. Saving your brain from Alzheimer's, and Depression, and Attention Deficit. These are real monsters. It may look innocent enough if you don't hang around the old folks homes, but if you go there and see the causalities of mental un-health, you quickly apprehend the poignancy of the topic. You've got two options:

Die young, or endure and hopefully enjoy the aging process. Aging is an exciting process as certain drives fall away and other motifs surface.

COOK IT UP

One wouldn't get away with the wrong measure of ingredients in a recipe or Science experiment. Here too we need to pump in the right numbers. When we do, we discover a statistical tsunami.

Alzheimer's was never heard of when I was a kid (my mother operated a nursing home) and is now literally omnipresent.

People call Alzheimer's an epidemic. ADHD is also an epidemic sweeping through our schools. Bi-polarity is everywhere.

Everywhere the dis-eased mind is evident. The best immunization is a mind with a plasticity fitness quotient, a mind not set in its ways but rather one that is fluid and flexible. You can explore divergence without it being a threat. You need a mind that rolls with the punches and stands its ground, with an evolving ideation that recognizes, when the stakes are high.

Looking at the reason behind the reason behind the reason behind, is what complexity is about. The confluences and manifestations are infinite. The sojourn is a sojourn into light.

DARK FLOW

<u>*FLOW*, a book by Mihaly Csikszentmihalyi , anticipated some of the issues that arise in the name of Entropy. What he says about the entropic brain is potentially the most earth-shattering of speculations. I couldn't help but read it and say Yeah!!!!! ABSOLOODLE!</u>

"One fact that does seem clear, however, is that the ability to make order out of chaos is not unique to psychological processes. In fact, according to some views of evolution, complex life forms depend for their existence on a capacity to extract energy out of entropy – to recycle waste into structured order. The Nobel

prize-winning chemist Elya Prigogine calls physical systems that harness energy which otherwise would be dispersed and lost in random motion 'dissipative structures,'" (Mihaly Csikszentmihalyi, Flow, p. 201).

The order that comes by way of chaos is a new order, a new type of order. Neurogenesis could source this entropic process. We can literally recycle the universe through our brains. No doubt this is the source of the archetypes.

The imagination is free of structures that parcel out thought. <u>Structures</u> of grammar and arithmetic are often too inherently uptight, too shackled within the organizational imperatives, too steadfastly within the normalization experience. The process of inherent modalities is simply under the radar and too a much part of us to separate our perception from. The uncertainty dismisses any attempt to reconcile to logistics. You can't corral uncertainty. Entropy is uncertainty. Uncertainty is fun. Some of my best friends are uncertainties.

If however, you realize entropy is temporary, rites of passage on the road to the unconscious, it is narratively pivotal. The unconscious and subconscious want to have their way with you.

In a near death experience, or an out-of-body-experience you wonder fundamentally whether you are a corporeal body. Your physical body seems an exercise in time and space. Similarly with any hallucinatory journey or journey into dementia the mind can travel body-free. Reconciliation works in mysterious ways. You lose yourself so you can find yourself.

Creativity is a natural consummation of reverie which is uncertainty personified. The personal openness to inspiration is what discovers and shapes a voice. For Salvador Dali the imagination was intentionally fused to paranoia to make the surreal real. On the edge of a razor blade things materialize.

Alzheimer's, I believe, is triggered by three things.

1) A lapse into sub-critical thought-processing, post adolescence, which carries the individual along into typified adult hood. The individual has learned to balance things, but the balance involves repression and masking of true feelings. The self is contrived to fit the measurement of others. This is standard Normalization.
2) The inability to relax when those first uncertainty episodes start chipping away at confidence can create a crisis of memory. Losing your keys can be epic. Each memory loss triggers doubt which triggers memory loss.
3) An event of extreme self-consciousness occurs when a person takes that look backwards over the shoulder and sees their life in a new way, outside Normalization criteria. The confusion over who

> they thought they were looms large and can lead to a psychological paralysis...a willingness to march on the spot. They often see this belated need to come to terms, well beyond them. They feel too old or psychologically weak. They don't know where to start.

They have never seen this 'uncertain' self before, making it difficult to go back to a self that has lost a vote of confidence. They hover in the indecisive.

There is more than enough energy to grab onto, in the dispossession cycle of the ego. This can easily represent loss of self or even death of self. Dissipation rates in dispossession structures are fuzzy fractals with wild fluctuations that say: sit up and take notice. You can't make sense of this the way you normally make sense of things. You are about to be swept away. This is when subcritical becomes critical. You feel your grip on reality loosening.

SOFT WIRED BRAIN

You may have seen a fellow named Michael Merzenich on PBS profiling the soft-wired brain. The brain is more soft-wired (plasticity susceptible) than hardwired. The opportunity in moving from subcritical to critical states offers creative opportunity galore. You can proceed with more conviction. Conviction fires and wires supernaturally. This is precisely what voice is about. Soft-wiring is an endless opportunity to migrate synaptic patterns to new brain areas. Add to this the subconscious uproar and you have all the makings of a watershed moment. A watershed moment, with salvation on the line in the form of existential self-realization, all focal pointing articulating individuation.

We're not talking focusing the mind. This is where Metternich obscures the point. The attention span is focus, but the larger focus, the third eye focus, is more spirit...it depends on lining up polarities. This means defocusing, not focusing. Often the normal focus, or attention span, has to step aside. You have to get out of your own way. The gravity of meaningfulness operates when the uptake inhibitors, like normalization-repression, dissipate. The dissipation frees up the self. Then at some point uncertainty is fun and liberating and navigable.

"Complexity consists of integration as well as differentiation. The task of the next decades and centuries is to realize this underdeveloped component of the mind," (Mihaly Csikszentmihalyi, Flow, p. 240).

This interface with creativity potentiation is what he has in mind. Unfortunately the Scientific secular world has no time for facts they don't like.

ARISTOTLE: THE BIRTHPLACE OF ART THEORY

Aristotle defined art as a trained ability to make something under the guidance of rational thought.

Training artists to do 'rationally' contrived art, that exhibits specificity in detailing, making it fundamentally an illustration was always in vogue. Pictures were rare and careful illustration was like photojournalism.

Arguments about Art and its place in the world go back a long way.

"In time, possessing an art collection became a badge of cultural sophistication, and the drive to acquire collections spread beyond the world of victorious generals …. By the 1st century BC a lively 'art world' had taken shape, populated not only by artists and collectors, but also by dealers and even forgers," (The Oxford Companion to Classical Civilization, p. 79).

Your social event and your Art collection might become the talk of the town. Discussions and insight followed.

Art oscillates between the ridiculous and the sublime. The ridiculous fades. The Art world itself is easily duped. A recent documentary featured a guy who had made hundreds of millions in art purchasing a stuffed goat. This was after the shark in a cage had made a big splash.

In Paris and Vienna there was a shift in consciousness. What came about was the art inspired by vision. Like the Shaman, the Artist opened self-consciousness to a new expansiveness. The parties where people stood around totally engulfed by a piece of art meant people were grappling with meaning. This was actually acceptable, and more than that, desirable. Art, it was discovered, could inspire people to adjust their awareness.

"In the late Hellenistic period a new theory of artistic creativity was developed in which certain artists, especially Phidias, were recognised as inspired visionaries whose insight (phantasia) and creative ability ... made them sages," (The Oxford Companion to Classical Civilization, p. 79).

Because we have lost the ability to engage art we have lost dimensionality in mind. Visionaries are no longer visionaries. That's why the education system has failed and why chest-pounding apes like Donald Trump can climb the latter of success. In the land of third eye blind, barbarians thrive.

Antimimon pneuma

"The end-result is a true *antimimon pneuma*, a false spirit of arrogance, hysteria, woolly-mindedness, criminal amorality, and doctrinaire fanaticism, a purveyor of shoddy spiritual goods, spurious art, philosophical stutterings, and utopian humbug, fit only to be fed wholesale to the mass man of today. That is what the post-

Christian spirit looks like," (David Lindorff, Pauli and Jung, p. 113).

Mass man is a single morphed creation a blob of information with a head and a tail.

Mass man gets everything in a nutshell. Pride cometh before a fall because a proud person has artificialized the mindscape.

You cannot rebuke the spirit of Christianity and remain Christian. Apostle Paul called out the Corinthians on this very issue. So-called Christians don't love their fellow men; they don't turn the other cheek. The parable about doing unto the least of men you do to Jesus is lightyears beyond them. That people pretend to be Christians without the necessary contriteness is typical.

These are Christians not Christ-ians. Much of organized religion is religion without meaning, religion cut off from earnestness. So-called Christians exemplifies this incoherence. They reflect only very little of what it means to be a follower of Christ type of Christian. Bombings in abortion clinics and shots fired through windows are 'testimonial' to the nature of their belief.

Is Jesus going to 'kill' to save unborn child? We're all God's children.

The bottom line is many are full of hatred and ready to shoot you rather than love you. This is directly because of their thwarted psychology.

WHAT ABOUT ART

What is Art?

Art is the dawning of the collective self-consciousness. Appearing on cave walls in early history it became a way for humans to look at themselves in action. As such it reflected evolution in civilization. Eventually one civilization could exhibit to another civilization and demonstrate where the collective mind was at. People capable of looking at themselves were capable of looking at a future.

Art tries to penetrate the contracted perception and rip it free of prejudice.

Art's transformative ability speaks to its sophistication and this creates complexity.

There is a difference between art saying a little and saying a lot. Creativity is risky.

We participate in an inter-subjective process transforming our consciousness to a new level of awareness. We look at the hunter on the cave wall and we recognize ourselves and what we are up to. Recognizing what we are up to has never been a perspective so needed. When we talk about the Mind's constructs we talk about jurisdiction and production methodology.

A Math Mind has jurisdiction in Math. Expertise comes from expertise. Almost the opposite is true in art. As a painter becomes a better illustrator, with more expertise, the temptation is to go into lockdown and showcase expertise not imagination. An artist finds a niche of acceptability.

Expertise is measureable and manageable because consensus is possible. I interviewed some artists yesterday. All started sketching young. Their sketching pleased people. Creativity was a sidebar.

Art is liberation. *Ways of Seeing*, as Berger has pointed out, become incorporated within the contextual realm.

Eventually we have textbooks and institutes and hierarchies and funding, and it's hardly any wonder why the information juggernaut industrializes the day to day.

The nature of this (sub-critical) mind versus a creative mind is a difference of jurisdiction. The creative mind tries to stir things up and see what happens. The Science mind tries to nail things down.

Jurisdiction is important because humans tend to falsify information to suit internal drives of which they are often barely aware. Einstein valued the *imagination* over *knowledge*. He differentiated between knowledge and imagination because there is a world of difference between them. He held the universe, in his imagination. He didn't get there by climbing an information ladder, or standing on the top of textbooks or peering over an organization chart.

The universe refracted in his imagination. It grew from nothing in his imagination to a whole understanding.

EVOLUTION ON TRIAL

Science was king because it delivered us from an angry god who made us pay for our sins. Hallelujah. The High priests, the money changers and the burnt offering rituals in the end were not about God. People despised such a God.

Science would push God off the front pages because objective truth was objective. God's status shifted, making 'God' into a superstitious primitive 'game' old people played. Young people tended to be secular. Everybody was rational and secular. Rational and primitive became opposites.

"Pauli, observing the outcome three centuries later, concluded that the rational perspective of science in the twentieth century had gone too far, to the point where it had lost a holistic view of reality," (David Lindorff, Pauli and Jung, p. 89).

Einstein had heaped praise on the young Pauli for his interpretation of Relativity which Pauli wrote for the Encyclopedia Britannica, at the ripe old age of 21.

Pauli was crossing the floor and going out of code when he confronted his self-hood. Scientists, especially those thrust into the spotlight, for the entire world to see, don't evaluate or second-guess their personal psychological reality.

Pauli had it made in the shade. He was a Nobel Prize winner.

Yet, Pauli was abnormal. He wanted to investigate the intangible realm of the psyche.

To stick one's head in a dogma is of course, evolutionary suicide but as illustrated, it happens every day, in all things human. It is all too normal. Your mind is trapped into a sequence of beliefs calibrated to fit the pattern of your life in a patterned socialization backdrop. Einstein said, being born human is like being born into a herd of stampeding buffalo. You're on the move even as your baby feet hit the ground. You get your act together and get up to speed in one breath or----you get trampled. To be on guard against the persistence of identity-shaping thoughts is the prerogative of only the few. Swimming against the current, going against the grain is hardly a piece of cake.

We are inundated. Few recognize the mesmerizing inertia, the seizure that captivates our existence and makes us into what we become.

Life itself, as big a picture as you can get, is a picture of chilling inertia. We have become an abomination.

We have gone smack-dab into an information blizzard and the wisdom of the ages is as a grain of salt in this chaos. It doesn't count because only a few can reference it. Thoughts project their own proclivity.

"Pauli's recognition that Kepler was stimulated by an archetypal image tallied with his own experience that creating a thought is not derived from the soulless intellect alone, but rather that 'intuition and the direction of attention play a considerable role in the development of concepts and ideas,'" (David Lindorff, Pauli and Jung, p. 86).

Directing our attention is a formidable task the moment we take it seriously. The information zone is archetypal. The monsters are real. They eat the mind. Intuition for most scientists is akin to clairvoyance and the Ouija board. Intuition is a projection of and through the imagination that takes on a special shape and a form of insistence.

What really got the hair up of fellow Scientists was a belief, held by Pauli, that psyche and energy and matter were fundamentally similar. Many people have been on board with this idea before but it remains on the fringes. The movement of energy through the psyche is powerful and potentially transformative.

A successful LSD trip is a feather in your cap because like the Ancient Mariner you have seen things you knew nothing about. Things that have registered with deep conviction and things you must pass on. THE LSD mind and the cannabis mind can launch a hyper-suggestive (plasticity-oriented) reality where the stupidest thing can become profound.

This isn't un-different from art. Art holds objects up to the light and simple can be profound. Happy accidents happen in ART. Vincent painted a masterpiece a day during his creative periods.

EVERY STEP YOU TAKE

"Jung found that a 'synchronicities' occurrence was accompanied by an emotional state fed by a deeply rooted (archetypal) energy, thereby connecting the synchronicity to the archetypal unconscious. He related the connection between psyche and matter to what he called the *psychoid* **factor, a quasi-psychic aspect of the archetype which is energized during a synchronicity. It is hypothetically the psychoid aspect of the archetype that makes the connection to matter. Pauli strongly supported this metaphysical assertion," (David Lindorff, Pauli and Jung, p. 100).**

MY PSYCHOID EXPERIENCE

Let me give you a personal example that I believe involves at the very least something extraordinary and peculiar. In 2003 I made a short documentary, or at least shot an hour of footage with a schizophrenic painter. In 2018 I was going back to my documentaries and tidying them up for posterity. For a month, I talked to my wife about this schizophrenia-diagnosed painter and how I should have thrown him a life line. Instead I only saw him that one time and didn't even know his last name. He had great ideas and great paintings. There was a lot of parental tension in the house and I left never to see him again. I knew him only from that one hour visit. When I saw the footage of Paul, I regretted not following up with him. He was on my mind.

Fifteen years had passed since I had seen Paul and this thinking about him was tied to my retrospective with my documentaries.

 My wife and I are at a Salvation Army store in Guelph. We were checking out at the cash when a guy comes over and asked if I did docs of artists.

It was Paul!

It was his first time in that store. I had been running him through my mind for a month but hadn't seen him in 15 years. And there he was like he had emerged physically from my thoughts. I should point out; I live in the country a good distance from where Paul lives in Guelph. Go figure. I now know his last name.

We exchanged numbers. I brought him to tour our place for a visit. I was excited, as I wasn't yet painting when we crossed paths originally. Now, like him. I was a painter. We visited his apartment. He's doing music, and painting. He's on meds but very much on his game...and something of a poster boy for recovery. Great art and great music.

We were grateful for once again being coughed up on the same shoreline. How does such co-ordination take place? For a month, Paul was running through my mind and voila he materialized. I believe psychoids had something or more probably everything to do with this. This is not the first time something like this has happened. Not by a longshot. If energy of some concoction didn't bring us together, then what was it?

I believe the same thing is made manifest across a variety of realms and within innumerable connections. Psychoids are everywhere.

Physicist Max Planck read an unknown patent clerk's piece of writing and recognized what it meant. This is an amazing thing.

Planck had no reason to give an unknown unaccredited non-physicist the time of day. But he did.

Without this connection through Planck no one would have paid Albert any mind at all. This too was a psychoid event, a transmission of a truly spooky psychoid action at a distance. A renowned physicist and an unknown patent clerk historically entwined. Brought into each other's spin, Einstein and Planck birthed Relativity. Planck, interestingly, shares Pauli's notion of energy, matter and psyche.

"I regard consciousness as fundamental. I regard matter as derivative from consciousness. We cannot get behind consciousness. Everything that we talk about, everything that we regard as existing, postulates consciousness," Max Planck, (Eben Alexander, Living in a Mindful Universe, p. 21).

Today there are a few courageous souls explicating the self-conscious or self-aware universe. Stephen Hawking's protégé, now at the Perimeter Institute, an hour from me, is on that bandwagon. Interviewed by William Shatner, Perimeter Institute's Neil Turok spoke to the notion of the self-aware, self-culminating, self-actualizing universe. We are materializing consciousness in how we culminate our understandings We are part of the materialization processing of the universe. It's a part of a universal medley. We are always on an engagement threshold. The self-aware engagement threshold is the most complex. It changes moment to moment.

It's dangerous. The slightest touch can collapse the wave. I remember my first handstand. Just as soon as I thought about it I collapsed. Our thinking invades our thinking all the time.

The physicist needs to know how to find the revelatory in his own psyche. The game is to not find the answer but to find the way, to find the answer. The way to find the way is to birth consciousness the sort that births ideas. The answer will pop out of a type of consciousness, a consciousness described as capable of giving birth. This 'type' of consciousness is rare in Science.

A Parkinson's study I've profiled in my writing saw a man develop the specific side-effects of the trial drug. He was worried about these side effects. After a hundred days of the study he found he had been given a placebo. Once again, and there are zillions of examples, thought manifests into material change. The worry about side-effects produced the exact side-effects. A sugar pill or his psyche, psychologized into being, concrete physical side-effects. Mind became matter. That's a very, very, big deal. The intangible became tangible.

What was planted in his head was an idea. The idea actualized.

That's the point here. Thought manifests and materializes. Stress-thoughts materialize in the body as factors in breathing, metabolism, posture, etc. then this in turn shapes the body's health, potentially, most frequently, opening it to dis-ease.

SCIENCE A FOOT IN COLD WATER

Mathematics giant and co-author of *Principia Mathematica*, Alfred North-Whitehead, saw scientists as disinterested in Metaphysics. It is, he said, a necessary role they must play or lose credibility.

Scientists are afraid of the psyche and afraid of admitting that they even have a psyche. They have lapsed into sub-criticality. They have a job. They have funding criteria. They have a Board of Directors.

"The brain exhibits more characteristics of criticality in the psychedelic than are apparent during normal waking consciousness …. The point is that the brain of adult modern-humans is in a settling rather than expanding phase,"

(The Entropic Brain: a theory of conscious states informed by neuroimaging research with psychedelic drugs, p. 3).

The dust is settling on the human experiment.

Indeed, Alfred North-Whitehead saw creativity as essential to the mind's construct. Everything besides the 'new' repudiates evolution. You become redundant. If you lock down and lock step reality, reality is a prison of the mind constructed by thoughts you repeat over and over till you don't know any better.

It's like being a guinea pig in a big version of that Parkinson's experiment documentary. You believe in the side-effects which are really mental projections actualizing statistically in your flesh

From heart disease to mental illness things actualize. Your whole reality can be contrived into being by self-perpetuating, tricks of the mind. Consciousness is tricked by distraction. Digital brains have no time to be conscious. They are committed to distraction. They love distraction. If for a moment they aren't distracted they are bored to death.

Exactly what Alfred North-Whitehead said is this, **"Creativity is the absolute principle of existence"**. This does not mean you have to be a Picasso. It means you have to have creativity as a place in your brain. The gap between what you've settled into becoming and what you need to survive is a creative manifestation.

In your own little way you need to open the valves to zero prescriptiveness. The human brain needs this. Prescriptiveness can motor on sub-critically forever. To adjust our modalities is what the quest for sanity entails.

Alfred North Whitehead talks of the" grandeur of achievement in the delicate adjustment of thought to thought," (Adventures of Ideas, p. 11).

Adjusting our thoughts allows us to maintain proper thresholds. Second guessing yourself can be an adjustment in process. I'm old. People think values change because you run out of juice. I say wisdom comes with difficulty and is treasured. Where I run out of juice is in fueling old polarities I've thankfully grown beyond. One can't feel smug without losing ground. It feels good when you leave behind a dumb-ass contrived piece of the self. Values change because you see through your motivations and through the subtext of your ulterior motives, your oppressive contextual imperatives that no longer prevail.

The evolution of thought is precisely that: the delicate adjustment of thought to thought. In a sense this becomes observable on psychedelics. You can control the speed and altitude. Delicate adjustment of thought seems tangible in a psychedelic experience. By navigating this way it moves the individual from being victim of his own thoughts, to being author of experience.

What happens after this is gravy. Because of plasticity you have to evolve to positive repositioning of the psyche. The first baby steps are more important than the masterpieces. Life recognizes the invitation of the moment. Each moment is in time and out of time, simultaneously. Each moment is corporeal and ethereal.

That's the trick. To be too engaged in time is to be unaware of the moment. In researching brain plasticity I see creativity as necessary to sanity. To fall into step with a world too much with us is to lose our bearings. To lose our bearings is to lose our coherence. Creativity is a lifeline you throw yourself. Creativity is life on your terms.

THE FIRST LADY DOESN'T CARE

We live in a very careless society. We collectively care less and less. The mind has its operatives put in place by society. Before you get a chance to participate in the nature of the interface, you are hook, line and sinker part of it. Jung and Pauli knew, it is not healthy for your psyche, if you never become you. If you keep pushing you down deep inside yourself you become increasingly ill at ease.

You are not a robot. You have needs outside the boundaries of who you are and how you think about yourself. Only you can open your eyes to your vista.

After it starts, this disenfranchisement of self, it's only a hiccup away from forgetting everything about yourself. The first signs of dementia are signs of divergence. The mental path and the physical path take different paths. In the long run Normalization was giver and the taker away.

Both of these thinkers (Pauli, Jung) would be able to make sense of it had they known about brain plasticity. For Pauli saving the psyche meant saving the self and the soul. For him the theme predated Christianity. The fact is, we are a product of our parents, our rulers and our schools. We all need to be saved from that. Why? We become indoctrinated with the attitude of the herd. We are infiltrated.

Because culture precludes who we are, we all need to be born again. You can see it as a Christian imperative or simply a neuroplasticity imperative.

When Wordsworth said the world is too much with us, he was referring to the world's invasiveness and its depravity. Its comings and goings are your comings and goings. You are infiltrated. You are set up by it. You live a life you never own.

"The world is too much with us; late and soon/Getting and spending, we lay waste our powers," (WW Sonnet).

When Blake lamented about 'adults' corralling the kids on the echoing green turnstiling them through school…. this is what he was talking about. A child is full of promise and potentiation thresholds. We shove the idea of who they are down their throats. We are ventriloquists. WE never give potentiation a chance to rise within their individuation. They puppet the culture never encouraged to learn beyond the cultural themes.

We reach in their heads and dial them to think the way we think they are supposed to think. School teaches you to think categorically. Authorities feed students the socialization schemata, the subtext of all curricula, for the sole reason, to make them compliant.

The education system has been constructing the minds of students valuing the academic catalogue, particularly Science and Mathematics over the experiential. Which if you sit down and think about it, isn't reasonable. So much is ruled out so early. It sets the stage for downsizing everything into an idea.

By filing them through the school, they are not the same after the **mind forged manacles** get through with them. They are tossed around like a salad. They are stood up in front of people. They are awarded. They are scolded. They are measured. They get their badges. They accumulate their failures. They thread the needle like everyone else.

Their minds will never work the same. Pink Floyd said the same thing in the movie THE WALL. Schools churn out medium grade hamburger.

Society wants you as another brick in the wall to substantiate its vision and reinforce its authority.

CATCHER IN THE RYE

Holden Caulfield, like William Blake, regretted the transition from innocence to experience. So much gets lost. What gets really lost is innocence. Bob Seger sings,

I wish I didn't know now what I didn't know then.

Holden couldn't bear to think of what the world would do to his little sister Phoebe. He wanted to be catcher in the rye, catching children before they fall into the abyss of adulthood. Phonies are everywhere in adulthood. Adults are fake news versions of the self. Holden despised adults. He sees the prostitute in the green dress, the guy with cheap suitcases and the guy who jumped out of the window with empathy.

Mark Chapman shot John Lennon because Lennon, he thought, had faked out. He had become a chintzy well-heeled aristocrat. Sincerity after celebrities become celebrities seems antithetical to what they have become.

Indeed, the entire enterprise of Education, Art and Science has been skewered by erroneous motifs and superficial themes. In the end a school curriculum is something the average person gets to keep them average. The average guy is not a threat to the state. School sizes you up, packages you and saddles you up to a future status you can't refute.

Art should have known better. So should Science and Education.

As Eliot says, we are distracted by distraction. Distraction is a trillion dollar business. We are driven to distraction. And now that we are there, in the heat of the battle, we are too distracted to figure out what education needs. We are pinned and wriggling on the wall of our own invention. The fault, Dear Brutus, is not in the stars, It's in ourselves.

MONDAY MONDAY, CAN'T TRUST THAT DAY

Emergent identity is central to creative individuals. Without creativity life becomes a knee-jerk reaction to a cascade of knee-jerk reactions. Successful people tend to be unreflective. It's easy to hide behind a successful persona. They have a good thing going. Isn't that what it's all about Alfie? He who has the biggest toys wins. Let's drink to that.

'Why' is not a serviceable question in many circles, in a pre-committed plasticity, fired and wired by habit and confirmed by daily ritual.

The mind becomes increasingly fraught with stress, tension, and self-destructive mental health issues. Life for many gets overwhelmingly embedded in frustration.

Many think we can link up with machines and we will be better. Better what? Better machines. That's the joke. If you are on the spectrum you don't know the difference.

Neuroscience can literally save us from Science but much of Neuroscience is wrongminded in its 'Scientific' approach.

When I hear of the experiments where psychedelic trippers are confined to a bed with a sleep-mask over their eyes it frightens me. I'm glad I didn't inaugurate my LSD trips that way.

I've had several LSD trips back my 20's and 30's. Some of these I will describe. By bending an experiment to fit established hypothesis theory we do injustice to what we can discover and to the how and why of the discovery. I will tell you of some of these so they may redefine what 'trip' means.

ZEN AND THE ART OF QUALITY

Happiness is complex. Studies (**The Structure of Psychological Well-being, Bradburn, 1969**) show that

Happiness and Unhappiness are independent of one another. That's precisely why we can be happy one moment and unhappy the next. We can think in two opposing directions at once.

The structure of psychological wellbeing is as individual as a person's finger prints. There are innumerable common shapes to experience but still we don't feel the same at weddings and funerals Each person brings their own memories towards an experience. A person isn't totally 100 percent happy and zero percent unhappy.

A walk in the park and a kiss in the dark have attached to them,

a very personal and very real subjective reality.

There is nothing more real to us than our subjectivity. By exploring subjectivity we go where no civilization has gone before, we go deep into the collective mind.

HIGHER VALUES and FAKE NEWS VALUES

Religion.

Christians believe in Santa Claus and the Easter Bunny and apple pie. They believe in the president, the Alamo, and the New York Yankees.

A stranger from a strange land would size us up easily. He would look at people congregating on Sundays…millions at the sports shrines and a few stragglers by comparison in the churches. This is a world full of zealots. They are religious zealots in the sense the team they support they support religiously. They jump up and down when someone hits a home run. They cry when they lose. This is pure fabrication of feelings and does not speak to the larger concerns of who we are subjectively.

Evangelist style churches are full of self-righteous hypocrites. What they believe in is anti-abortion and racism and Wall Street and corporate greed. They believe in tail-gate parties and on Sunday the day designated by God to remain Holy, they watch the Holy game of Football. I find it worrisome, that Oprah who I greatly admire is unwary of many of these false prophets in red Lamborghinis. All these guys white and black are slick. They aren't real. If Jesus walked into these churches he would be flabbergasted.

Jesus wouldn't spend a second in their presence. He's the guy who chased the money changers out of the temple. Can you imagine Jesus in a Lamborghini cruising? Can you imagine Jesus shooting up an abortion clinic? If you can you're more fucked up than you think you are.

Jesus doesn't want a Grammy or an Oscar or any material reality. He wants to save your soul.

It's the Evangelicals supporting a serial adulterer, who beds porn-stars and playmates and who wants to rule the world. Trump is a water-boarder, a child-killer, an un-empathic not to mention foul mouthed, blasphemer. Yet the Christian Soldiers line up behind him. Why do white people and the evangelicals support him? Because he's white. Because, like Hitler he keeps it stupid and simple. He appeals to basic uncultivated, uncultured instincts. He appeals to their inner will to power. He appeals to biceps and 'white' arrogance. Simple and stupid are the shackles of totalitarianism.

THE COMFORTABLE PEW

Everywhere the Catholic Church exists there has been sexual misconduct. There have been thousands of cases of priests exploiting their power Just yesterday (Feb. 2019) the Pope recognized nuns used as sex slaves by priests. One can only assume God was not their motivation to go into the priesthood. The hypocrisy everywhere apparent riddles our society with falseness.

In her memoir, *The Spiral Staircase,* Karen Armstrong portrays her psychologically twisted journey into nun-hood. Thank God for Karen Armstrong who emerged as the most perceptive person on the planet when it comes to discourses about things religious .

The way the mind works depends entirely on how we fire and wire. If you fire and wire lust your mind isn't on God. Capacities are fired and wired into being. Our subjectivity and what we look at and how we look at it is important and crucial to any honest spirituality. We gravitate to being the most comfortable self we can become, the self we can get away with. Life is a hustle.

Francis Bacon, perhaps the last meaningful painter talked of the lapse in our capacity to see the new.

"They buy when the artist is famous – and perhaps no longer doing his best work. But when there is something marvellous and new, they don't see it," (Francis Bacon: A Retrospective Exhibition, p. 44).

This is precisely why the Peggy Guggenheims are rare.

Everywhere the craft usurps the art. Precision and focus replace expansiveness and vision.

Travelling through a Dali or a Picasso or can make you wonder what is going on. There is popular art and there is real art. There is decorous art and there is Sublime art. There is Art that glances off you and Art that sticks.

The confusion is a confusion sustained by Art school graduates trying to pretend they can learn how to be creative. Being creative is not the same as being talented. Talented means you have proficiency in draughtsmanship. Teachers patted you on the back because you could draw.

The ones who get to art school get there because they are good at sketching not good at being creative. To be creative means you can dial the combination that yields continuous chance. The combination depends on having the appropriate humility.

The mystery of accident is the mystery of the self-unfolding. Feeling the self unfold is the best kick of all.

Utopia

Plato had it right. For authority figures and political leadership we need philosopher kings who earn very little money, who aren't impressed with material empowerment. They don't need the image-building a red Lamborghini brings.

Some people through empathy want to help, no strings attached. It's these people we need in government.

Empathy is feeling that is conjured inside the self, it is the heart that connects to another self, or a whole population of selves. It is a direct mirroring experience. People with low levels of mirror neurons are not capacitated for inter-subjectivity. Fortunately anyone can remodel the brain with increased capacitation.

It's all about adjusting our thoughts and resonating with things of the spirit.

PAULI'S NIGHT MARE

Feeling is something Wolfgang Pauli never thought his father had. Wolfgang had trouble connecting with his father. The family situation was very Hamlet-like in a way, except in Pauli's case, the father betrays the mother, by hastily putting her in the rear view mirror.

The son finds this chilling. Pauli's mother had killed herself at age 48. Pauli's father married a woman Pauli's age.

Then Pauli's wife left. Anima and Animus issues were central or Pauli as he reconstructed himself.

If Pauli stuck to his guns, to science, he'd hold up, faking it like everyone else. He could hide behind his Nobel-Prize winning persona.

But in his soul searching he couldn't hide. This would be a facilitation of his own dismal failure. He needed to sort himself out.

For a self-realizing human being, emotions are strategic to wellbeing. A healthy amygdala is for the best. Pauli had to find his inner compass, get his alchemy right. That meant facilitating the best psyche resources, which meant learning from repetitive psychological and emotional mistakes.

FLEEING THE BEDROOM

Feeling is being extricated from human existence. The December 2018 cover story in *The Atlantic* is entitled: **The Sex Recession.** People are shying away from people and intimacy is under siege. People are no longer at ease in another's presence.

Of course people have every reason to be afraid of sex these days. Pornography has distorted what men are looking for in sex. In light of the Me-too movement sexual exploitation is centre stage yet mentally unhealthy intrapsychic enactments occur everywhere, incessantly. These diminish selfhood and stop self-realization in its tracks. Once the opportunity for enriched human intimacy, sex is now more than ever a polarized reality. The fall out is existential and real.

Deprived of confidence in intimacy, humans become psychotic like in the monkey mothering experiments. As our society succumbs to the spectrum initiatives we have little attention span for finding our emotional compass and relating to another person. People are dismissive or afraid of romance because like in *Rainman*, a hug can be threatening. An unknown inner sense of self seems unobtainable. If you can't connect with yourself how you do connect to someone else? When the world becomes a void, where empathy and love fail, baby steps into intimacy are needed. Encouragement and respect and re-enchantment are prerequisite. Hardly anyone has time for it.

There is a great Banksy painting with silhouettes of lovers in an embrace looking over their 'partner's' shoulder to check their I-phones.

As TS Eliot says, NOTHING CONNECTS WITH NOTHING.

Without connection we are lost soul wandering a Wasteland without any compass.

We are condemned more and more to disconnect. We all move towards Autism and lower inter-subjectivity content in our lives; because of more face to screen and less face to face. It's the world with us.

An emotion-limited human won't know how to handle emotion. We won't know what hug means person to person. When you go screen to screen, you leave how you inter-personalize behind. The mirror neuron part of the brain goes undernourished. Eventually you forget how to personalize the relationship not only with others but with yourself.

We don't know each other as deeply nowadays and we lose the capacity for inter-subjectivity. Intimacy for Rainman is something he can't handle. It's beyond his scope. It sends him into a disorientating spin. That's where society is going as characterized in this Atlantic Monthly article. People aren't willing to risk intimacy.

Any inter-subjective intimacy will eventually be unnavigable. There is something excruciatingly discomfiting about feeling out of sorts with yourself. Navigating another person's emotional needs requires that we tap into our most complex resources. The concept of Catharsis is about identifying with another human's fear and heartbreak to evolve one's capacity- not only for others but for self.

Like Paul on the road to Damascus, all things can change in a miraculous moment, an epiphany can crack open a life time vista. Thunder and lightning can transform the self. This cascade of change can be fired and wired in a quickening unlike anything else neurologically. People can change who they are and what they value, in an instant, in the twinkling of an eye. Many such stories are legendary. Change is an archetypal event.

"In fact, a religious conversion may even be forced upon consciousness and, if resisted and refused, may make the person quite ill. Such seems to have been the basis of Sigmund Freud's own neurosis, the direct result of setting up bulwarks to keep out archetypal/religious material that was trying to come through from unconscious/spirit reality. Saint Paul is the prototypal example of how archetypal forces of the unconscious can burst through and force themselves overwhelmingly onto a split-off, dissociated consciousness," (Robert B. Clarke, An Order Outside Time, p. xv).

Regardless whether epiphany is fast or slow the necessity for change is part of our essence. You need to manage your portfolio of modalities. This means keeping up the 'good' fight for justice and balance and access to neurogenesis. In tending to one's mind, the psychodynamics need to evolve expansively. The mind is not meant to be locked into habits and be tied down to the same features. Patterning creates membranes of foreclosure. Foreclosure creates pressure. When the dam breaks it can be like full speed ahead chaos. Paul the Apostle was blind for three days. Nothing could be more disorienting than to have the script you were following, shredded. 3 days of blindness.

Oedipus becomes blind and suffers greatly. In the end is not of this world and its political turmoil. There is a crack of thunder and Oedipus disappears. All indications point to a supernatural event.

'**Why do thou persecuteth me**?' came the voice at the moment Saul/Paul sees the light.

Saul became Paul. Paul went from a bounty hunter pursuing Christians to a fisher of men. He would meet a worse fate than Jesus.

Why are people willing to be martyrs?

What they cling to is otherworldly and non-quantifiable and hence non-rational.

To grasp the notion of spectrum one side leaning towards empathy, creativity, and metaphor the other side leaning towards autism and a lack of inter-subjectivity, we need to see what is happening to us.

I've mentioned how a child's chance of being autistic increases if both parents are math professors. What is happening to us all is a detachment through personalization and a diminishing of attention span, particularly for the exercise of things human. As we lean towards the mathematics and science education we diminish empathy and conceptual awareness. The logistics oriented rational mind triumphs. That's how we play ourselves false. The logical rational mind has jurisdiction over mind territory it should be subservient to.

THE BRAINMAN

Daniel Tammet, autistic Savant known as *the Brainman*, can recite pi without any mistakes for four hours. That's one accurate piece of machinery in your head, if you can do that. His story is truly amazing and books reveal a great articulation of the Spectrum. One book, Born on a Blue Day, deals with his progression when he couldn't find his way from one classroom to the next.

Daniel lacks inter-subjectivity and imagination. He has to carry a photograph of his partner so he can match up, with the guy (his partner) who comes to pick him up at the airport. Precision he has. An inter-subjective hypothetical mind is beyond him.

Camus' Meursault is a portrait of a man estranged from his own existence. This sort of existential estrangement is rampant now. More and more of us feel estranged. Meursault was not impacted by his mother's death and passed through his own murder trial unmolested by feelings. Without feelings to anchor you contextually you lose sight of the self you need to become. Worse by far is to phony up. Meursault isn't going to fake it. Normalization kills the unconscious.

Psychotics can pass lie detector tests because they have no conscience. A conscience is in large part an empathy quotient thing. The more you can identify with others the more you experience their pain, the more conscience rendering that goes on.

I saw this on a Forensic show recently, where a murderer (eventually found out) was let go because he sailed through the lie detector test.

If you are a worry-able person you could worry about failing the test and your 'truth' might seem like a lie. What is being measured is your nervousness quotient.

To JS/07/m/378

Was he free? Was he happy?

The question is absurd, says poet D H Auden. Auden (I saw him do a reading at York) characterized the trivial pursuit nature of people's lives.

> **Except for War, till the day he retired/He worked in a factory and never got fired/…..his reactions to advertisements were normal in every way/….he had everything necessary to Modern Man/A phonograph, a radio, a car and a Frigidaire.** (WH Auden)

The unknown citizen is compliant and does what is expected of him. His is not to reason why, his is but to do and die. Happiness and freedom have no meaning to an JS. He is unknown to himself an x variable with the prescriptiveness of an automaton. He fits in. He accepts Normalization, no reason not to. At a certain place on the spectrum freedom and happiness are non-appreciable. Misinterpretation happens easily. The most twisted word in our history comes in the name of freedom.

HAZING

St. Mike's private school in nearby Toronto hit the news recently. Hazing hits the news. This is what hazing is about: killing empathy, empathy, and love. Holden Caulfield sizes up the boys school culture prevalent in the schools he attended. Marc Lewis, addict turned neuroscientist, was shipped to such a school from his home in Toronto at age 15.

James Castle is assaulted and bullied to his death in the private school setting in The Catcher in the Rye.

Hazing is a group think phenomena, the mob turning into an aggressive like-minded, blob. It's the stuff lynch mobs were made of. It's also much characterized by sheep in wolf's clothing bureaucrats.

Hazing is about killing the emotions. It's about killing empathy. It's about doubling down on the male extreme prerogative. It's in the domain of the Salem Witch Trials and the Spanish Inquisition. It is about people turning on other people. It is people captivated by the most perverse of psychologies. Like in *Lord of the Flies* when the young

British schoolkids revert to uncivilized violence all hell can break loose given a little momentum.. People get beaten to death during these hazing incidents.

Nobody cares as a young man gets sodomized with a broom handle. To a spectator even on social media, the milieu implicates, kills you. It kills us all. It condemns the human experiment.

Your internal spectrum and its fundamental 'usage' in terms of empathy establish awareness and inter-subjectivity levels. Inter-subjectivity enhances perception by mobilizing it. Empathy can't help but reach out. Catharsis can rattle the soul. In the absence of a Social milieu Inter-subjectivity grows through reading and cultivation of thresholds for sensitivity and empathy. In books you get to choose your friends.

19th Nervous Breakdown

Every dissociation is troubling and unsettling but often necessary when the time comes to reset the compass. It's how we feel out the Three pound universe. Like groping around in the dark you have no idea what to expect. A life outside the expectancy cycle will free up the hard drive.

Every day you do a sit up or push up you do it with a different self, more or less like yesterday's self, but incrementally positioned differently. Waves or phases can leapfrog you ahead or backwards.

easy to forget that you fire and wire each day into being. Each day your bicep expresses itself anew. Your incumbent self is that much older and that much different. That's why old age comes as a shock. You can't monitor the changes. Suddenly you are what you've been slowly becoming.

This can't be me/must be my double, sings Leonard.

There is no biological explanation for a lot that goes on in the land of endorphins, peptides and make-belief. With the placebo effect, where there is no definitive way we can regulate placebo to our advantage other than believing. This is why any brain attention works favourably. If you monitor your brain even with brain gyms your brain enervates because of the attention. Igniting the brain within such limited causality miscues the brain on things more abstract.

It's this intangible world that is so biological yet so much more. The Mind in so many ways is a battle field, not only in discerning fake from true, but in regulating non specificity-prone matrixes. Such matrixes are beyond your cognitive insight but the Spirit can set you up to navigate and morph accordingly. You have a you that's on the backburner and it casts a shadow. The ambiguous and ill-defined are real in your elemental constitution. In the end it comes down to symbolic interactionism. If sugar pills 'represent' healing then that is what is going on. Rather than garnering suspicion we should be all hands on deck, to figure out the potential of neurogenesis. Watching videos of back anatomy or knee anatomy healing can induce healing.

WHEEL OF FORTUNE

Our expectations seem to project an affirmation of self when things go right. When we are on a roll, things fall our way, in our favour. Something similar might be at work with placebo. If you know life is a perilous journey with bumps and craters it comes as no surprise that things evolve.

After all we don't expect a defeatist to react well to a sugar pill. He or she might, but it seems that good health reaps what it sows, because of a positive psychological outlook. Positive belief is not the power of positive thinking in Norman Peale's sense, which can lead to emotional misrepresentation. Sticking an artificial smile on your face can grow into something you hate about yourself. Still, a smile on your face is usually an asset to your own self-concept.

The Entropic Brain paper, by speculating on their own version of the spectrum, throws a great deal of light on the topic of human consciousness. What do imaginings do in the mind structure? What goes on when we encounter the unconscious because a drug has revealed our inners to us? Who are we when all hell breaks loose? And who are we when we emerge when we've gone through hell for a heavenly cause?

Alzheimer's, I believe, is a life style illness. We don't tend to the right things in life. We think that rapid cognition is a good sign of someone with it. Nobody evaluates the existential because it has never been part of the conversation.

There is a style of thinking that goes with the life-style incorporated will to power.

Dementia comes about because we indulge the wrong social dynamic and fail to include truthful strategies. Truthful strategies are assumed to be what everyone is up to. This is where consciousness and conscience come in. If you have core principles you are more centered than someone who is just an information bundle. Your strategies for other minds will include the deep resource mirroring offers us.

To avoid dementia it's a good idea to face off with uncertainty rather than allowing it to gang up on you in the golden years. Dealing with levels of uncertainty is like immunization. You get used to it. It doesn't freak you out because it is a fact of life.

64 thousand dollar question

These are becoming the most meaningful questions we can ask. Where is sanity? How do we find it?

How do things get amplified? How do we pump up the tires of our hopefulness? How do we rescue sanity? How do we keep our heads when all about are losing theirs? How do we, like the Ancient Mariner, live to tell the tale?

The mind is inflatable in that it can fire and wire what is essentially new brain. NEUROGENESIS.

Brand spanking new brain not dedicated to any materialization means it can go wherever the body needs it. It can heal you. It can inform you beyond the traffic jam in your mind.

SPONTANEOUS HEALING

I've misplaced Andrew Weil's *Spontaneous Healing*. In it, he describes spontaneous healing situations which suggest miraculous transformations, which in the end are material and physical. Weil ponders why this type of healing can't be accessed more frequently. If we could channel neurogenesis we might be able to transform our physical selves. We have no real idea of how far we could evolve because we are held back by the traditional male mind, a mind that loops out in such territory. We have no real grasp of our healing power.

People with strokes and other issues have been physically altered by migrating brain firing. This should be exciting news but it's lost on the mainstream.

If such miracles of plasticity can happen when our backs are against the wall what about in healthy individuals?

What are the possibilities for everyday plasticity and/or psychedelic participation? What psycho-kinetics could be revealed with due diligence. What imaging could be used to accelerate healing?

Wake up people. The end is nigh. Life is passing by without us giving it a second thought. You can't escape your mental torture and migrate firing and wiring to your advantage unless you potentiate threshold. You can't potentiate big time unless you believe big time.

You can escape the tedium of the daily treadmill.

But for too many, when it comes right down to it, you feel too perplexed, too paralyzed and too tired.

THE BRITISH EMPIRE

Once upon a time, the high tide and green grass, of empire beckoned. The Rolling Stones and Mick Jagger sang about a guy on TV telling him, **how white his shirt should be and falsifying his imagination**.

Perverting the imagination by seducing the collective attention span is everyday McLuhan-aged fact now. The Stones were onto something. So was Dylan when he sang, *'The Times They Are A-Changin'.'*

Having your imagination falsified is brainwash. Falsification is inherent in what is called maturational settling. Maturational settling is normalization. Things are taken for granted for so long that one thing commonly mistaken for another becomes established.

Currently in the UK the number one cause of death for males 50 and under is suicide.

Happiness is more elusive than it has ever been

Amit Goswami points out in *The Self-Aware Universe* and in his work he calls *Quantum Healing* the degrees of magic we might expect. Science, to my knowledge, does not embrace him.

Rejection is even more the case in where a representation erroneously stands in for fact. Art is institutionalized, where the academic's mind encloses within its vista ideas about art that are erroneous. Neuroscience is unequivocal in distinguishing creativity and originality.

"Looking on, physically and observationally speaking is not the least bit like doing the having in the first place. The bat is having its sonar sensation, feeling as it feels when doing its echo location trick; the human chiropterologist who surveys the bats' neuroanatomy, however minutely, cannot have that feeling no matter what. (And since the bat does not talk at all, much less indulge in phenomenological reporting, this means the chiropterologist can never know what it is like to have the sonar

sensation). A human being, looking at an empty but deeply cyan-colored display on an RGB monitor has an intense visual sensation, but a neurophysiologist monitoring that subject's brain from a good safe distance has nothing of the sort," (James E. Tomberlin, editor, Philosophical Perspectives, 4 Action Theory and Philosophy of Mind, 1990, p. 111).

Being plugged into creativity is a powerful thing. This is precisely why the artist and real subconscious exploration is so important. It's a different beast than what curators think they do when they curate. It's not marginally different. It is profoundly different.

It is existentially different!!

It's so different many see a link between madness and creativity. Vincent Van Gogh was nothing like the lusty drunk in the movie *Lust for Life*. He was fluent in French, Dutch, English and German. He read voluminously. Many artists however like Jim Morrison, and Kurt Cobain were self-destructive. Like Rimbaud and Lord Byron they met untimely ends.

To date, the Zurich Kunst Museum in Zurich and the Musée d'Orsay in Paris are my favourite galleries. The latter has a number of Vincent's works.

In 2015 my wife and I were in Zurich.

I hadn't tuned into Giacometti as an artist before seeing his work in Zurich. It is of course the same Zurich where Pauli and Jung made psychic history. There was bound to be a lot of psyche in the air. I was thrilled by Giacometti's work. It was, like my own work, psychological.

Surveying his work and life and researching him I came to the conclusion his death was the culmination of repressed energy. His work and his patented style was all he could do. He couldn't budge himself. He imploded with a creative force that couldn't escape his mortal coil.

Every time he started to diverge he was unhappy with what he was doing. He fell into old patterns. He was trapped in what Amit Goswami calls old memory. Old memory can become difficult if you can't get out from under its shadow. It can crush you. Old memory is the weight that eventually brings one down. We need to navigate memory and fashion it into a negotiated understanding. Carrying it forward as a learning experience is far better than carrying the dead weight of an unreconciled past. The last month of Giacometti's life the struggle would surface in a portrait he started and revised over and over and over. He was trapped in the gap between what he had been and what he needed to become.

It's good to remind oneself that images before print, before magazines and newspapers were rare things. Now our brains try to cope with image avalanche. So what, you might say? Firing and wiring strategies aren't going to work unless you think them through. It's only a hundred years the brain has had to deal with image constructs and flash card memories. The human brain is continually being information bombarded. Hard-drives in the brain are fragmenting.

You haven't defragmented your brain unless you have tended to its organization.

Commercials like the hypnopaedic training in *Brave New World* get through our defences. Each commercial is an infinitesimally small way in which the mind is manipulated and the imagination eradicated and supplanted by consumerist motifs, images and symbols. We are indoctrinated. Symbolic interaction is consumer driven.

(He can't be a man if he doesn't smoke—Rolling Stones)

The Marlborough man was the Man. Male ideation has always been between a stone and a hard place. Stanley Kowalski crying Stella was a man possessed by an idea of himself of who he had to be.

I live not too far from the small town where I grew up. My friend's mother resides in the expensive senior residence in town. The lawyers and business people that ran our town when I was young are there with her, playing bridge.

She was president of the golf club, the curling club and socialized with the town's upper crust.

Now she lives in the senior dream home, the Taj Mahal for retirement refuges.

Many people here are, however,

losing their marbles.

I mention this for a couple of reasons:

1) I believe the brains that our society collectively fires and wires are an erroneous brain, a brain that gives up in the stretch. In the long run Normalization fucks us over and it is hard to recover.

2) I wonder if dementia goes in waves. Let's say a person whose mind seems to exemplify got-it -together-ness, who plays bridge well—suddenly shows signs of dementia. Would this be a catalyst?

If somebody you thought had a strong mind and turns around and loses it, it would shake your confidence. Mental illness has a ripple effect. We will see a lot of this in the decade ahead.

Confidence in your mental faculties comes from understanding how you think. Practice does not make perfect. There is no perfect. There is only better and worse. We were taught to think by life style rules. He who lives by the sword dies by the sword.

It's easy to lose confidence in one's self when others seemingly more solid lose their way. Is this also a psychoid activity a negative convergence of psychic details when several people go over the falls, in the same month? I pose this in a humorous way not to be humorous but to give a visual sense of marbles being spilled, the cascade of dissociation. Entropy unleashed.

We adapt to sociological expectations and this is the forcefulness that shapes us by default. Alfred North-Whitehead characterizes the delusion that is perpetually ours.

"The force of its peculiar adaptation (generalized idea formats) fit the concrete circumstances of a particular age. It is a hidden driving force, haunting humanity, and ever appearing in specialized guise as compulsory an action by reason of its appeal to the uneasy conscience of the age."

The concrete circumstance of our age is what I've been talking about. Depersonalization, alienation from intimacy, normalized rigidity etc.... There is truly something scary about how stupid we are.

Like in Buddhism you are given the very sort of life you have so you can work on what needs to be worked on. It is an individuation problem.

We get what we deserve. We get superficial leaders because we are superficial. People with no faith in a belief system tend to get desperate and grab at straws. Donald Trump is such a straw. That is the adaptation strategy of many worldwide. We are our own worst enemy. It's similar to developing side-effects appropriate to our fear. We need to respond well to the consequence of challenge.

You can't, not drift, towards the order of things. The world gets us coming and going. The order of things pulls us like a magnet. **Here we go round the prickly pear at 5 o'clock in the morning**, to paraphrase Eliot. We'll do anything to keep up with the Jones who are now the Kardashian family. For contemporary humankind the grandeur of the wider truth is eclipsed totally by the omnipresence of digital invasiveness. This is our force of adaptation.

This is a complex way of saying that cultural themes prevail and exhibit the self-ordered dysfunctionality we see everywhere. The fault is not in the stars it's in ourselves Shakespeare said. It's what we deserve. That doesn't make it easier. By ordering our socializing structures and our mental constructs in the name of education, in the name of how things have been done, we are duped by group-think. Education it turns out is bad for the mind. My wife who is in the education system told me today of STEM AND STEAM. The last decade and a half of my teaching career the principal was a Science-major jock. This was typical throughout the Board. The whole system leans in the direction of STEM: SCIENCE, TECHNOLOGY, ENGINEERING, MATHEMATICS.

This moves us towards Autism on the spectrum.

STEAM is a new movement re-introducing the notion of art and creativity. It may be too little too late.

Our generalized malaise comes from this inherent inability to value what needs to be valued. Again and again as we frame it up, humans follow the wrong pathways. We become "unknown" to our true selves. We shy away from our own depth. Willy Loman is too busy keeping his head above water to get an overview of his own retroactive suicide. Willy never measured up to success. He was always under the gun to sell, and to be a success like Uncle Ben.

So too, Holden Caulfield, in a world that boxed him in to its criteria and measurements Holden was an alien. He was an oddball. Everywhere throughout literature there are oddballs and rebels real and fictitious. The song, **He's a Rebel because he doesn't do what everybody else does**, gets it right. Once you don't toe the line you have enemies in the Greek chorus.

Non-compliance with Normalization doesn't sit well with the old folks. Any deviation, even positive and artistic is 'wrong' because the conformist doctrine is integral and uninformed. It is something that has to be rooted out regularly like weeds in a garden. From *Town without Pity* to *Harper Valley PTA* the typified social faults rely on the perpetuation of pettiness and ignorance. Easy to be hard.

Standing UP AGAINST THE STATUS QUO: Jesus Christ, Gandhi, Malcolm X. James Dean, Marlon Brando, Cool Hand Luke. We aren't stupid but we fail to follow up on lessons learned about how social strictures can circumvent a more open, truthful, psychodynamic reality. We don't take entertainment to heart. We go untouched. Conformity rules. Normalization is poison.

As Jeanette Winterston's mother says, **"Why do you want to be happy when you could be normal?"** Normalization has gobbled up everything and everyone. Like in Sodom and Gomorrah the debacle is pervasive. No one wants to say goodbye and accompany Lot and his wife on the purification journey.

No sitcoms; can't imagine such a place. Who would want to live there?

Normalization is not working. Every weekend in several places in the world people march and protest governments. There is potentially in chaos a tipping point. It might be the yellow vests or the women's march.

Upheaval is around the corner. There are no value benchmarks.

But guaranteed Normal is a ticket to eventual dissociation, to gnashing of teeth.. In the next 20 years, legions of people will become mindless. Like in Saramago's *Blindness* novel, everything will be chaos. Insanity will win by a landslide. When a lot of people start losing their marbles that will be a tipping point.

CERN

CERN is often seen as the current capital city of Science.

When it came to publishing the papers and letters of Nobel Prize winning, king-of-physicists, Wolfgang Pauli, they had quandaries over the format, particularly questioning whether Pauli's letters to Carl Jung should be included. They thought Pauli's interest in dreams and the occult were somehow beneath Science and could tarnish the collection. Science, despite centuries of psychiatry, cannot threshold with an embrace of the mind. Scientists are block heads like a Rubik's cube.

That's why I say Science is on the spectrum and not up for the future. They are stuck in a groove of pre-condition and precognition sponsored by the old paradigm and its funding tentacles.

As I said, in 2015 my wife and I went to Switzerland. We visited Einstein's apartment in Bern and the Einstein Museum in Zurich.

We didn't go to Cern. I had applied there for an artist in residence tenure and got virtually no response except the automatic e-mail.

I guess what they wanted was an art installation that gives some tourists something to look at besides the particle smash-up derby. (Might as well put the Simpsons on TV display).

What I wanted to do at Cern was stir up creativity, empathy, insight with 30 different workshops from personal video account journals, to Pollock splash and dash. To be creative you have to stir up the creative juices. Then you can think and imagine freely.

By birthing the consciousness that births ideas, I could have saved them from early onset petrification. You birth the birth zone and THEN you see what happens. Alas, Science like Art has no use for creativity.

Where Science is on the spectrum they don't have the range to apprehend what they need to apprehend. From where they are situated they can't grapple with deficiencies in their imagination. You can't hit what you can't see. They are at a dead end. There's no Max Planck. There is no Einstein. There is no event horizon that allows for deviation from what is.

CRY BABY

Descriptions of childish rants portray Pauli as a man out of control. He was a mess. But then Pauli became a changed man by wanting to evolve. Nothing illustrates what is pathetic about the Science mind more than this debate. A man tries to find his way and the petty ones throw rotten tomatoes.

From now to doomsday it will be like this - people incapable of seeing outside the ingrained perspective.

Psychiatry saved Pauli; put Humpty back together as a better man.

The Science minds are the second most overrated minds in the universe, the first being world leaders. Science minds are axiomatic to what is.

I reiterate. Pauli went from a volatile self-indulgent bastard with an emotional IQ of a 10 year old, to a subjectively evolved human being.

What upset Science is the evolved position Pauli took, as reflected in these quotations and the ones above. For your average joe - straightjacket - scientist these positions are untenable because they are untenable in science dogma. Scientists are patriotic when it comes to saluting the tangible and ignoring really deeply reflective thinking.

"The layman always means when he says 'reality' that he is speaking of something self-evidently he knows, whereas to me it seems the most important and exceedingly difficult task of our time is to work on the construction of a new idea of reality."

"Einstein has a feeling for the central order of things."

"Both of us seem to agree that the future of Jung's ideas is not with therapy but with a Unitarian, holistic concept of nature and the position of man in it."

"When one analyses the pre-conscious step to concepts, one always finds ideas which consist of 'symbolic images'."   WOLFGANG PAULI

Science refuses to believe psychology exists or that creativity is a non-sequential and non-correlative 'reality'. This is what Pauli called, synchronous, acausal and aperceptual   reality. Literally Science refuses to admit that it has a brain. **Until Science addresses the shortcomings of science, true exploration will isotope into the lowest common denominators of funding explanations.** This is Fascist and no climate for opportunistic creative quantum leaps. To face the truly big questions one needs a multidimensional mind. Some of it involves outposts and logical constructs chasing down a decimal place, but much of it doesn't.

Those are the facts.

To pretend that we know the universe is out there, material and measureable, is heresy. That view reflects nothing of what recent developments in physics tells us. We add up in ways that are more, than the sum of our decimal places. Brain illustrates this as MIND. Mind travels outwards from the brain and into events.

Mind is psychoid-oriented, boundless, and ethereal, a fluid compilation of different types of information and manifestations. Information cross-references and cross-embodies as mirror neurons engage the interpersonal in feel-see conceptual energy.

At the entrance of the Van Gogh Foundation in Amsterdam is Vincent's quote about needing to give vent to one's creativity. To dismiss this energy is to fire and wire dissociation and madness.

"Dissociated are self-other representations, interpersonally derived traumas, and whole or fragmented self-states that are too overwhelming or entirely do not fit with the existing sense of self. Such intolerable states need to be removed from the conscious awareness for one to emotionally and psychically survive," (Efrat Ginot, The Neuropsychology of the Unconscious, p. xxxix).

We need to work it through us.

Jung and Pauli hoped the day would arrive when Jungian principles would prevail and human beings would own up to the complexity and complementarity of being human.

For scientists short on symbolism and imaging their concentric self-affirming reality is textbook. And they do it by the book. They are puppets to paradigm.

We are talking about spheres of experience. Pauli was willing to go where today's Science pulls up short.

NEEDLE IN A HAYSTACK

I'm looking for some vacuum bags I put in my editing room. It's a mess. Finding a needle in a haystack would be much easier. The thing is: something tells me I'm looking in the wrong room. If I am looking in the wrong room I won't find what I'm looking for. Not if I look forever. Science, much of the time, is looking in the wrong room. A little imagination would reveal conceptual short sightedness. (Maybe my blindness is my excuse for not doing the vacuuming-not beyond me)

I see this Entropic Brain surmise, revelatory of the very topography of neurology that is pivotal in brain mapping. Science can't grapple with the brain issues even given the 20 pages or so, referencing study after study. There is none so blind as those who refuse to see. And the refusal to see is generational, hierarchical and spectral. People get stuck in a particular way of seeing, a particular thought structured paradigm.

There is lot to be learned here. To the authors of THE ENTROPIC BRAIN: Science probably didn't notice your paper. Even something as 'science' fortified as this paper, is too much for Science to accept. Science doesn't go there. It all boils down to consciousness. It seems many are called but are few chosen when it comes to mindfulness and metaphoric constructs. Even neuroscience, which should by now know better, probably didn't offer up more than a nod and a wink to *The Entropic Brain*. In the system the wheels are oiled. Science is set it in its ways. Maturational settling profiles in individuals and within interfaces throughout the field of Science and all of humanity.

In the very functioning premises of the human mind, the very nature of the necessary mapping comes into view in *The Entropic Brain* paper. We need to flush out contours and shapes of shapes. The answer is not in atomizing detail but in conjuring intuition. With uptake inhibitors and potentiation thresholds, the moving parts don't necessarily add up to a clear view. Up and down, off and on become confluence issues.

Does blood flow sometimes shut off parts of the brain? How do we piece together a workable composite revealing the spectrum of possibilities? Where does Entropy figure into the comings and goings?

But first …

UP IN SMOKE

Canada, where I live, has recently legalized cannabis. Cannabis and creativity go way back. Poets and painters have recognized how it is easier to fire and wire in a creative way when marijuana gets them 'high.' Plasticity is more active. Cannabis is a Launchpad for the imagination.

The three CNN docs on Cannabis may strain belief because of the universality of the success of the drug. It seems to help everything under the sun. Whether stopping seizures in babies or curing alcoholics, ADHD, or whatever the drug seems to work. There is one simple reason: Plasticity. Plasticity is enhanced on cannabis and firing and wiring is liberated by the drug. Your endorphins, peptides and immune system relax. You get high. You leave your troubles behind. What you do with it from there is up to you.

And there is no brain degeneration like with alcohol. Short term memory loss, not so bad—it's what you want to lose because you are a prisoner of short term memory. This is where your anxiety is. This is also a memory facilitation that recognizes Normalization constraint, so you deserve a holiday.

You become a space cadet, which shouldn't be alarming—you are diverging from the normal orbit. This gives your mind a break. Maturation settling has intent to settle you in your ways. It ties us up in knots if we are dysfunctional, and we are all dysfunctional.

The pressure to be a consumer, to be other than a dud at the Christmas Party or New Year's, to be a somebody, on Facebook is omnipresent in the world of social media, and that is increasingly the world we live in.

Marijuana can cause a psychotic reaction in novice situations because of the dissociation from being in step with the normal co-ordinates, the internalized imperatives. This dissociation is entropy. It is divergence.

The 'white' backlash, against grass is often Evangelical. They would pepper their own kids with ADHD drugs like Ritalin or get their kids on antidepressants rather than confront their prejudice about cannabis.

Antidepressants, Ritalin type drugs, and the host of others get endorsement. Opioids have killed thousands. LSD killed one person, a CIA agent whose buddies slipped him LSD unbeknownst to him. You cannot die of an overdose of LSD.

There are so many kids on the mental 'un-health' spectrum that public and for that matter, private schools, can't cope. This is because the ignorant consumer-driven establishment endorses big pharmacy. Like feeding kids to the Minotaur we perpetually dispose our children to corporate greed getting them hooked on anti-depressants, or whatever. We are our own worst enemy.

The contours of the shaping forces are there for any socially acceptable initiative. Everyone wants to be confirmed as part of the crowd, part of the herd. Drug marts are everywhere. Many of those drugs are killing us. But the White establishment thinks it can pick its poison.

To fit in takes work. The cookie cutter will lop off the edges. To earn a living takes work. To face the hassles at work, takes effort. To stay on the good side of your spouse, your kids, your parents, all takes work. The stresses we face affect our immune systems and paralyze endorphins and peptides. We cramp up. We bend over. We get exhausted. Our posture, our gait, our metabolism and the strength of our hearts reflect the embeddedness of who we are. Grass gives us a break, a mental vacation and our body is happy and healing is in the air. We vibrate with the morning. We wonder lonely as a cloud. We want to write a poem. Such is the prejudice against it that many will refute the obvious need to get a buzz on.

Neil Young sings: **It's painful coming down ... no use running away**. Leonard Cohen says, **"and wasn't it a long way down**." The depth within our own feelings when we fall into ourselves is staggeringly real.

GOOD VIBRATIONS

The discoverer of LSD, Alfred Hoffman, lived to age 102 and was lecturing at age 100. He took LSD regularly into his 80's. LSD enhances divergent thinking. Cannabis is LSD's little brother or sister.

Personally I would like to organize public plasticity events. Painting, poetry writing, dance, drumming circles, Tai Chi, even sailing events, etc. Ironically many of things to do would involve traditional things, hop scotch, sack races, hammering a nail into a block of wood, square dances. Do si do.

We have with the cannabis drug an option for stimulus—to be introspective, to be creative, and to find a voice. Using the window of opportunity for profound escalation and amplification of selfhood is what enlivened plasticity offers. In any group the energy becomes synergy.

My wife won't forgive me for giving up on the Monsanto trek. We went to the top above the boulders only to find a different route went further. It was a hot day and felt like a 150 degrees. Monsanto Portugal is the site of the earliest civilization. People have homes where caves used to be. We stayed nearby at Hotel Fonte Santa. This place would make a beautiful plasticity centre. All drugs are legal in Portugal.

We can take advantage of this. It would be about love, understanding and inter-subjective exploration. Thousands find marijuana a stimulant that is life-affirming and life-enhancing. Those with an uncreditable relationship with their own subconscious are most afraid. This includes Evangelicals who don't love their neighbours and are conflicted because of sin.

Their disturbance is so strong they are flooding the letters to the editor section of the local paper. CAS (Canadian Automobile Association) has taken upon itself to televise people playing table tennis with cannabis simulation goggles to demonstrate inebriation.

This reality distortion is BS.

What a crock.

I guarantee you I can play table tennis or real tennis as well or better, after smoking grass. If you are paranoid the opposite can be the case. You can become ultra-wired and nervous. Generally you will have a better physics feel of your body in motion. It can be exhilarating.

Alcohol can also be liberating but it works as a depressant and it messes your memory and your timing. You fall off a stool because you don't understand your body. With alcohol you can't punch without telegraphing it and when you do, it's a hay-bailer. Alcohol kills brain cells and you have to become an alcoholic to get the same mileage, down the road. The road to addiction starts with a business drink or two. For me I got tired of hangovers and throwing up. Afraid of crossing the Atlantic the first time I drank 3 or 4 Scotch. Upon landing in Gatwick I soon succumbed to a hangover. It felt like I had an axe in my head.

BEAUTIFUL LOSERS

Leonard Cohen wrote a novel during a hashish binge. Carl Sagan smoked grass every day. Grass doesn't turn you into a zombie. It can turn you into a gazelle, a writer, a filmmaker, a creator. The thing is you have to let yourself be free.

LSD appealed to Stanley Kubrick, Jim Morrison, Bob Dylan, Steve Jobs and Silicon Valley inhabitants. Throwing off the shackles of maturational settling is precisely what drugs can do for us. For me 'grass 'is no indoor party drug. It can be hard to get comfortable with people because one is more emotionally and psychologically apprehensible. Faking it is not desirable. The line between seeing things and making them up can be blurred intentionally. I remember certain parties decades ago where edginess vibes could develop.

Vibes.

Most parties had good vibes like Woodstock, but some had bad vibes, particularly if there was a group of drinkers around or speeders. Macho guys were threatened by grass. A confrontation with the unconscious is unheard of, not in their vocabulary. Not on their radar.

We imbibe the status quo growing up knowing no better. Attitudes become structures. Structures become fortresses.

Cannabis has a place in psychedelic experimentation. Cannabis in conjunction with LSD offered the ultimate combination for me, personally. One gets a gentle ride to the end of an LSD trip if one smokes a joint, at the halfway mark; say 4 hours in to an LSD 'trip'. This slight maneuvering can be felt, made graphic in its physicality, its stratification. This is in part the magical thinking that comes naturally and the magic carpet ride that follows. You learn altitude. It is fun. It is exhilarating to escape from this world.

People used to crash after LSD trips. Trips were psychically engaging and intense. This in itself could be fun. Nothing could be closer to the bone than a white knuckle 'trip' through the psyche. The catharsis of a trip and liberation from the maturational settling can take some time to feel in its entirety. The impact can last for eternity. A person can walk away from smoking or drinking addictions, or depression or any number of bad things while tripping. Plasticity is migrating.

High is high. It's higher than the people at the bus stop. It's above the stench of commerce and the pollution of values at asphalt level. It's a hot air balloon up up and away.

It's above the daily grind. This bird's eye view is special beyond special, and it allows for the opportunity to pick and choose. You can fly eight miles high.

One picks and chooses with more scrutiny with more respect for the long term self. People forget how to read the writing on the wall because they are looking elsewhere, and they lose the language of reflective thought. Cannabis launch-pads reflective thought. For many that is a brand new language, a new conveyance modality in their own understanding.

REEFER MADNESS

Most people have heard about the movie *Reefer Madness*. It shows people smoking the 'devil's weed' and going insane. A white woman appears to be in the drug's power and simultaneously captivated by unholy sexual urges. Marijuana paranoia was drummed up by White culture. Thousands of Blacks went to prison. Just as thought constructs are inherited they are diffused into our collective bloodstream. Many in my family are against cannabis—it isn't them. This drug is a medicine better than what you get at the pharmacy. Much current hysteria about legalization stems from this erroneous picture we have collectively subsumed. Much of it involves White prejudice and the ensuing mythology. Cannabis was a drug that gave you long hair and put a drum in your hand. It is un-capitalistic.

It's hard to be two-faced on drugs. The experience will find you out.

The CIA experimented with LSD for 2 reasons:

1) They thought it might be a truth serum. And for sure there are aspects of the experience that make an individual want to own up; you want to come clean. It's more complex than that of course. The unconscious poses some new questions and you have to scramble to identify experience.

2) The other reason has been exposed in experiments recently made the subject of lawsuits and documentaries. It occurred here, in Canada, in Montreal at McGill University. People were subjected to horrific scenarios. The CIA, on Canadian soil, attempted to literally erase the minds of 'guinea pig individuals' and supplant the old mind with a new mind, a CIA designed mind. As I said, horrific stories have emerged.

The head of this experimentation was an SS stylized guy. People on staff were terrified of him.

Alcohol causes 3 million deaths a year. I know I said this. It remains information we don't process. Liver disease, dementia, broken homes—this is the history of alcohol. Still, we grew up a high ball culture.

Before legalization of cannabis the local paper painted dire scenes from concerned citizens. As I mentioned, every week more and more, reefer mythology cropped up in letters to the editor. There would be, or so they predicted, carnage on the roadways. Now 4 months later there have been no accidents.

THE POINTLESS FORCE

The whole point is the freedom of expression and pursuit of happiness. Einstein said the chief problem with society is in confusing means and ends. The modus operandi of grass is observation not aggression, clarity not confusion. Anything else is a bummer.

If you want to get the world to sing in perfect harmony: grass can do that.

I remember doing an acting course put on by Theatre Ontario at Laurentian university. My first extended scene in front of classmates involved a Canadian play (BATTERING RAM), with a wheel chaired character (me) jealous of his wife's whereabouts. There were sound effects that had to emanate from my boogie box at exactly the right time or our scene would be laughable not serious. On the way to the drama room, my co-star, an interesting woman, and I, smoked a joint. The scene involved a block of memorized lines of course plus props and the essential and timely sound effects. We pulled it off perfectly. The altered state actually made it more believable. We "got into it", the characterization of the script.

A drunk wouldn't be able to do that. I've been drunk. I know. Think *A Star is Born* when you think drunk. Drunk can be fun especially whirling around the dance floor. Drunk catches up with you.

Indeed, if, unlike the *Reefer Madness* scene, there was a white guy like Dean Martin, with a martini in his hand, the threat to society would seem entirely different. We package the devil and make believe it is something it isn't. It's always inconvenient or unmarketable to package the truth. Interestingly Santa Claus characterization traces its way back to Falstaff (a drinker)and Mephistopheles. Santa is a contrivance to put Jesus out of the picture, so the correlation may not be misplaced.

I myself had psychological rigidity from my Pentecostal background. The first time I smoked grass I started to shake. This alternately freaked me out and made me laugh. I didn't know whether to shit or go blind, as they used to say in my neck of the woods.

When people have a psychotic episode it is a projection of their own fear. That's precisely why it can't be taken lightly.

It is an expectation of side-effects like in the Parkinson's experiment. If you think you are unstable, think you are going to freak out, you likely will. But you won't lose your mind.

Marijuana opens the antennae that project from your nervous system outwards. Our character armour regulates our nervous system keeping us cramped in some surrogate fight or flight persona.

TORONTO THE ELECTRIC CIRCUS

In a crowd of all strangers your vibes can be awakened positively or negatively. I remember walking along Yonge Street in Toronto before a 3 Dog Night Concert and just about everywhere one looked there were 'weird-looking' people. By this I mean normal faces distorting as if representing archetypes throughout a range of Modigliani brokenness, dark and light. Faces falling out of dark and light.

Unfortunately the night was coincident with High School Graduation Commencement where Mr. McLaughlin was scheduled to hand me the History Award.

My wife wonders why I would mention this. I want to acknowledge what he did for me. Thank God for Mr. McLaughlin who was one of handful of teachers throughout my schooling who took an interest in my abilities.

On LSD You're wired to a more 'vibrational' sensitive awareness. Things can go sour but my experience with this was negligible. Green speckled, purple microdot, California sunshine, window pane and blotter all had slightly different realities to offer. They were fun in their own way.

I GOT AN IDEA LET'S GO OUTSIDE: *EASY RIDER*

In *Easy Rider* they go outside (on LSD) and walk through a graveyard.

Life and death can get up close and personal on LSD. Of course one may feel one's personal space entrapped and need to get out catching one's breath. One-on-one with nature is the best. Aldous Huxley's account is right on. Movement is an experience. Colours are unmatchable. The atmosphere is thick but ethereal and light.

This is the risk. An obsessive-compulsive can require 5 times a psychedelic dose to get a drug experience through to the psyche. It is a massive defense system that does not want to be found out. Depending on your character armour you will have an easier or harder time with the drug. It is genuinely profound either way.

We settle into ourselves. We don't want forgotten things stirred up. We don't want dull roots catalogued and enumerated. Character armour is a foot wide. Dislocation, disorientation, Dissolution can cause profound anxiety. That's a risk factor. The risk hypes the threshold making epiphany possible. Another risk factor is altitude. You get high. Too high. Looking over a panorama of global history high: the flow of history is part of the experience. Of course, surveying the teleological aspects of the ancient self can be disorienting.

That's the point.

Watching with a sense of life pulsing in your brains, watching an ant climbing a blade of grass can be enthralling. A butterfly can be heavenly sign. The uniqueness of experience is fleshed out, the moment suffused with what it means to you and your connection with things. This is a very special self-incarnated reality. The quantum wave un-collapses. The question how did I get here is an ominously present one? Like, with the Ancient Mariner who ends up adrift on the timeless seas, there is a lesson to be learned, and a tale to be told. The lesson might be there is no lesson. It is archetypal. Individual sets out of the voyage of her life. The voyage is called life.

Off course you begin to wonder if you are ever coming back down —

I'm a Rocket Man and *Ground Control to Major Tom;* all make amazing sense when you are flying high.

Is that so bad?

Maturational settling settles in and we hang up our wings.

"April is the cruelest month, breeding/Lilacs out of the dead land, mixing/Memory and desire, stirring/ dull roots with spring rain," (TS ELIOT)

The couch potato doesn't want to move. Discomfiture is unavoidably uncomfortable. Couch potatoes grow roots into the furniture. The entire reality can take root. The brain goes to seed.

BLAZING SADDLES

Any paranoia feeds the plasticity because fear fires and wires real fast for obvious 'fight-or-flight reasons. Fight or flight. That's a big decision to be caught in the middle of. The thing is to find the balance as mindfulness. Ride out the turbulence. Let entropy take you. In sub-critical daily agenda reality balance isn't negotiable. Here it is. You are under the gun of a culture that wants you to pull your weight. Pulling your weight is the way things are done. Einstein called this the cult of efficiency. You are boxed in by a million alienating features. Then boom, you break on through.

On drugs, shared metaphor can easily turn into theatre. A description can lead to shared interface. Most of my cannabis or LSD use was with no one else, at the most two or three sharers of the experience. As I said, a crowd can dice things up, making for alienation vibes that are palpable. But beyond this the self gets drawn into a crowd and that can make it a different experience.

TRIPS

When I lived in a basement apartment in Toronto, with a wonderful Italian family up above, we convinced each other we were mice. Magdalena and Luigi were people and we weren't. We were mice. It seemed to go on and on …. and at one point we felt it might really happen: we might turn into mice. So we stopped. I've heard of groups sharing a hallucination. I know four people who shared a bad trip. They kept looking in the mirror for their bearings and for reassurance. Not a good choice as I will soon illustrate. This is the weird Narnia-in-the-closet, Indian-in-the cupboard, effect of LSD. The imagination can swallow you and everything becomes archetypal. Like in Castaneda's profiles in *Art of Dreaming* something begins innocently as barely a curiosity then animates into a liveable animated universe. Not unlike Hesse's Magic Theatre in *Steppenwolf*. The experiences are engulfing, riveting… and ultimately for me had a carefree fleetingness to them. It can also be profound. Sometimes it can be harrowing. Harrowing is the most profound.

What is the alternative?

Waiting: a dis-ease

A FETISH, AN UNCONTROLLABLE URGE TO DO NOTHING IN THE FACE OF A PRESSING DANGER.

It is easy to see something like Beckett's *Endgame* and *Waiting for Godot* being conceived on acid. I've seen *Waiting for Godot* four times. Once was on acid (at York University Burton Auditorium) about 6 hours into my trip-a comfortable place. It was hilarious on LSD. Many things you encounter like LP covers in the sixties declared a whole different level of experience. 'Are you experienced?' sang Jimi Hendrix.

There was a dividing line between those who had tripped and those who hadn't.

ONE GIANT STEP FOR MANKIND

My first LSD experience was at a campground. It was mind blowing. It truly was.

I told myself throughout to balance my fear. If Rod (my friend) can keep it together I assured myself that I could.

Or can you? It was in serious doubt. The orange tent emanated a colour field as thick as mist.

At one point I was losing it. The shoreline of reality was a distant figment of my consciousness. I climbed on the roof of the car. It was summer and warm. We were at a camp spot no one nearby. On the roof I stretched out and tried to bring my mind back to some semblance of translatability. The sky is usually a calming thing.

There were many stars. It was a starry starry night. In this case the stars were red and green and flashing on and off.

Like the Northern Lights. As I tried desperately to sort this out I had an out-of-body experience. I was up near the tree tops looking down at myself stretched out on the car roof. This freaked me out.

My fear collapsed the experience. I fell back into my physical body, a different body from my astral body. I wish now I had had the courage to deal with a wonderful opportunity, for trans orbital flight. I chickened out. I never had such a legitimate out of body experience ever again in my life.

FEAR 101

It's always useful to relativize fear. My brother loves motorcycles, but horses put the fear of the Lord into him. My wife is afraid (sort-of) of spiders. If there is a bat in the house she has no fear. She likes bats. She builds them bat houses. She nonchalantly puts a container over a bat and slides a thin plastic sheet to close it then delivers said bat outdoors. It only happened once but she was truly impressive saving the old bat. I do this with spiders. She tells me she told me how to do this. I'm not sure if this is a false memory of hers or not.

FLASH??? BOOM///BAM

Fear and surprise go hand in hand. They both can startle us. Surprise is always part of an LSD adventure. Expecting the unexpected is the expectation. Accepting surprise on its own terms helps more surprise to happen. If you panic and shut it down, like I did my only ever out of body experience, you miss out. There is choice. You don't have to go over the Falls in a barrel, if you believe it's all up to you. You are within a certain idea, captain of your ship. Your mind is willing to believe that. It is willing to give you the benefit of the doubt.

During a psychedelic trip the brain exhibits more characteristics of criticality because more is at stake. Your mind seems at stake. You can make more at stake to the extent you desire.

I liked to exercise. I'm no jogger but I liked to go jogging on LSD, listening to my Walkman. There is a potential for kinesthetic liberation. I believe these leg stimulators used by paralysis victims could enhance their situation given what LSD or cannabis can do. Same with the new 'sight' techniques.

CANADIAN WINTER

One night, Christmas Eve, (both of us post-divorce) a friend and I went out to a cottage in the bush off HWY 136. We had done LSD an hour before. The cottage (my brother leased) was locked and I was wearing city slicker clothes. It was freezing. We were 400 yards from our vehicles. I was desperate. I circled my lips and regulated my breathing tightening muscles and diaphragm but focusing on the breath. I acclimatized.

Again, this is stuff Tibetan Monks can do and I did it on LSD.

Till this day I consider it a miracle that I didn't freeze to death. I had a little jacket on no hat or muffs. The point is: THE PSYCHKINETIC power of an LSD integrated mind-body suggests profound potential. The current experiments need to incorporate the psychokinetic realm. I believe that meditator's realm can be accessed with instantaneous results.

Losing your mind and body is one of those prospects you encounter during an experience so obviously a great deal is up for grabs.

Suddenly 'existentiality' comes into focus. Looking at things existentially without the fill-in the blanks reality, is precisely a stage where thinking diverges and differentiates.

What are you here for? You'll be asked.

We get isolated from existential information by the perpetual upgrades and downloads (*we are the stuffed men we are the hollow men:* TS Eliot) -- Entertainment, politics and sports. We create a head-gear mentality in us. LSD takes the helmet off. And the gloves.

Another Trip

Once I was at the Orangeville reservoir lake cemetery on LSD. My parents are buried in that cemetery now but they weren't way back then. For some reason my wife finds this sentence hilarious.

It was and is a beautiful place. In the Fall with the blazing orange and red maples reflected in the water, it is a visually gratifying setting. In this instance it was no doubt simply a place away far from the maddening crowd.

However, a dark moment descended on me. Everything went lights out....totally black and I knew this was a public place and I didn't want to be a public event. I certainly didn't want to be on the front pages of our small town newspapers. I certainly didn't want my family to know that I was experimenting with dangerous drugs. What I did was I willed the darkness away which made me feel like Joshua. And it's a point of arbitration that stayed with me. It was power I had going forward. It's magic.

I willed the blackness away. Like pulling a switch the light came up. Like alchemical magic. It's important to realize how pivotal your thoughts are in precipitating what happens.

It's important to remember the psychokinetic power you have. It's very much like the movie version of *The Tempest*, the Mazursky one with John Cassavetes, Susan Sarandon and Molly Ringwald.

Prospero, the architect, points out the window and says **show me the magic** and lightning rips the sky as if attached to his finger tip. Creativity drugs can immerse you in a down the rabbit hole, quantum experience. You can materialize a great deal of firing and wiring with one trip. It can give you a leg up on tomorrow.

DETACHED SOULS

To be confounded is overwhelming. This is where mental illness comes from. The mind loses faith in itself. Life is a treadmill passing through the same scenery every day and it can go off the rails when confounded. After a few residence moves and the street scenery fades into the non-particular, a street with no name is where you are.. A person who becomes embodied only within a contrived reality can easily be duped. The scenery changes but the mind fails to take notice.

When the pathway diverges the individual FINDS HIMSELF ON A HORSE WITH NO NAME IN A DESERT WITH NO NAME. It's a difficult situation to contain with common sense.

The singular point of existential literature has to do with the self beyond the daily ritual the program of being. To get trapped in a heap of circumstantial evidence is the human reality. To get a picture of how you fit into the mix is difficult. By underestimating what the threat is in 'brain' terms, is important. Most would prefer to go to the grave rather than have it out with the self.

As Leonard Cohen says; **YOU LIVE A LIFE YOU NEVER CHOOSE.**

In the *Entropy* article they reference the brain's functionality when non-ordinary states prevail. When life complicates beyond resolution one can be propelled into a non-ordinary state. It doesn't take drugs to get you disoriented. Life does that. An altered state can be a place you go during a divorce. It can be where you go after being bullied at school.

The brain is enervated, percolating its plasticity, potentiating, and coming on line with a critical, existentially manifest, non-ordinary self. And it feels great. It can be a profound antidote to depression.

"That's the whole trouble, when you are feeling very depressed, you can't even think," says Holden Caulfield (the Catcher in the Rye, p. 91).

You may diffract into dissociative personality disorder formerly known as multiple personality disorder. A psychedelic experience can dove tail realities.

Art is the conviction that your voice must answer the call. No other voice will do. This easier said than done.

When *The Entropic Brain* writers reference **a maximum number of metastable states or transiently stable and unstable states** this is what creativity is about. Creativity is about finding a way out. Neither stability nor instability are desirable and one can't be extricated from the other. The transient entropy pulls you into its nature. The stability grows like a Phoenix from the ashes. Transience resolves itself in fundamental ways.

This isn't internet surfing, this is imagination surfing. There is an ocean of infinite possibility; possibility reeled in again and again as superimposed correlations dovetail into manageable confluence. As psyche meets image.

At any rate, back to the risk.

Many people go off the rails in life. Conformity acts as an action of massive repression. People seemingly solid performers are at a loss when tossed off their donkey by a subconscious manifestation of dislocation. Divergence and dislocation can be particularly difficult for the conformist.

"I want to argue that in the history of modern art the entropic becomes dominant, to the extent that modern art increasingly seems like a failure of creative nerve, or rather, more pointedly, creative imagination and creative intuition – imaginative intuition, one might say …. Creative imagination…is replaced by pandering to everyday social interests, usually stripped of their affective resonance and existential implications – their human dimension …. It is ultimately a self-righteous preoccupation, calling for a new conformity and simplicity in its conception of the social truth. Indeed, the simpler the message the better, for a simple message is easier to communicate to the masses than a dielectrically complex one. We are

effacing the collapse of the sense of what it means to be human, more pointedly, of all feeling for what it is like to be inside another human being – an empathic, humanistic goal of modern art since romanticism," (Donald Kuspit, The End of Art, p. 41-42).

Many conformists don't see themselves as a person who could go off the rails, or even pandering to a subliminal reality. Hence when uncertainty materializes; it seems as insurmountable as it is improbable. By repressing the authenticity of the individual we cater to our mental demise. In reducing art to a marketing proposal we destroy our collective mind and usurp the ability to see ourselves. We are hypocrites and we like it that way.

Many are eaten alive by a downward spiral of circumstance. Going insane is entropy. Entropy is break down. Broken people and broken planet. You can't put some Humptys back together again. Ironically the culprit is often rigidity. Rigidity is the perfect costume for entropy. Things are falling apart but under a mask of coherence.

To counteract rigidity, you have to eat humble pie and reckon with yourself. You have to do this honestly and contritely. You have to admit you are wrong. You have to evolve through the dimensionality of what it means to be human.

A few years ago I was I thought on my deathbed.

I wanted to apologize to a former girlfriend for how ugly and petty I got during our wind down. I called her, surprised she still was at the same number. I left an apologetic message.

Then, I felt foolish and wanted to apologize for intruding into her life.

The person I owed the apology to was no longer there and it was wrong of me to make her life retroactive in the instance of listening to the message.

If you can mend bridges that should be mended, that's great. The important thing is internally. Uncertainty is everywhere. In a self-aware universe culminating as we culminate. There is a preference for wholeness. Jung and Pauli saw this as the archetypal journey. When you come back you see yourself in a different light, you see yourself for the first time. And you see things you want to change. This can be a cathartic experience, and can revolutionize the personality. Going back to the daily grind may require mental adjustments. At least you have a better sense of what you are getting yourself into.

All around you and all the while, the periphery is shrinking to small screen Pacifiers. This shrinks the depth of field and the nature of being allocated re: attention span.

BOYS WILL BE BOYS BOMBS WILL BE BOMBS

I was going to leave this out but I'm including it. It makes no sense to be a mountaintop guru. There are processes at work. We have to some extent absorb the pain in the world to stay human.

20,000 people have died in each of the last 8 years in Syria but Christians extend no Jesus love. This is the post-Christian world on display.

Everywhere, technocracy is performing lobotomies on the young by digitalizing adolescent brains, prescriptively.

The turnstile reality of impermanence is catching up with everyone. The persistence of the disintegration of memory is eating away at us.

No benchmarks. Nothing permanently addressed by the psyche to govern itself. It's easy to feel abandoned like an information cork bobbing in an ocean of information. Conscience-less leads to unconsciousness.

HOW CAN GRASS HELP?

The group synergy created by a shared joint can translate well into music, into painting etc. in discussion it can be a breeding ground for shared metaphor, even a shared hyper-reality.

Neurogenesis

The same hyper-suggestibility that can throw gasoline on the fire of paranoia can ignite magical collaboration.

It seems all at one's fingertips. Like life itself. To get more elbow room in the mind, and more breathing room in the heart, a change has got to come. This is easier said than done. The selfhood that we are extricating from involves the old anchors in the form of irrefutable habit.

As TS Eliot would say,

> **'And when I am pinned and wriggling on the wall,
> then how should I presume
> To spit out all the butt-ends of my days and ways.'**

Exactly

A lot of people are excited by changing the brain for the better. We are attached to ourselves and often stick to whatever coherence we can muster.

We realize a lot of people are falling through the cracks. The **'slings and arrows of outrageous fortune'** can make or break us.

CHANGE

Michael Pollan's book, *How to Change Your Mind* and Jordan Peterson's *12 Steps* are just two books, amidst a host of books which are offering up the same message. Change!!!! Or your system will become outdated and innerness estranged.

It's too easy to become depersonalized. You will be cut loose from the vitality of your own being.

Because of what habit diminishes and life choice bracketing precludes we get lost in the labyrinth and the oxygen is sucked out of us.

A stratified organized mind is a simplification that can work against the identity's identity.

Holden laments a teacher whose motto was *simplify and unify*. Somethings he suggests, you can't simplify. A certain type of mind cannot accept that somethings doesn't boil down into something else.

The functionalism and utilitarianism of life gets us in a half nelson before we are knee-high to a grasshopper.

We get it intravenous. We imbibe socialized reality through our parents our teachers, our preachers, and politicians. And we get it all wrong. And we get stuck.

The threat of self-hood apocalypse is no small threat. We create a fort to defend the self, and psychologically we strap on character armour to prevent self-annihilation. When a psychedelic drug comes along and shatters an idea of self in the private and intimate setting of mind, things change.

The idea package that you've subscribed to since day one, is no longer valid, barely worthy of facilitating a daily agenda. You can feel vulnerable and unhinged. You can drown.

No wonder, then, the name entropic brain.

Entropy is the breaking down of things to perhaps, irretrievable form. Cars rust. Buildings crumble. Fruit rots. We get old and there is rust in our joints and our minds flat line.

Life dies.

When a glass shatters, it's not likely to ever come back together. Things fall apart and they remain in disarray. Moreover it seems the universe itself is entropy-prone, a point not lost on the self-aware universe. We have to watch our step.

Life itself is anti-entropy and so is Art. But entropy is the author of uncertainty and spinner of possibility.

Guys and girls planting hundreds of trees a day in forestry get 'claw' hand from gripping the seedling trees and planting them. Our minds fashion a grip that details the nature of our grip-styled consciousness. They grip only what they grip.

Most minds going into their 60's play it safe. They have a sort of carpel tunnel vision. A painter may crunch the mind into feasibility, exercising a conservative syndrome in executing choice. It seems innocent enough but at the end of the endeavour plasticity has conformed to a new idea of itself which is an old idea.

Soon-to-be seniors have learned about the small print. They believe strongly that the rest of life is best organized so that things are expected and don't catch one off guard. Going into your sixties you can be such a creature of habit that your metabolism assumes a certain rhythm, your outlook, a certain scope.

Your gait and posture and your face on face recognition software can be interpreted.

IT'S ALL RIGHT MA, I'M ONLY DYING

The imagination is dying in the collective consciousness. Pauli and North-Whitehead are stating in no uncertain terms that the transformative power of the psyche is at the core of evolution. Yet we have buried the prospect for change in our thematic applications. It is what it is, in the ways of the world. By constraining ourselves to traditional and typical frames of reference we imprison the psyche and the psyche pays the price.

Wittgenstein and Gödel were towering figures in Mathematics who see Mathematics as axiomatic, a thing unto itself, a language. And not as a map of the universe.

Neurogenesis

Big as mathematics knowledge is, it is small in the big picture. It has its own radius.

Mathematicians use the myth of math's invincibility to self-deny a rigorous soulful exploration of self. Lock step, rote-learners with zero Empathy and zero conceptual awareness, are not leaders in thought processing. They are with the program. They are the program.

They will not do drugs that elevate plasticity towards the imagination. They are afraid.

They'd sooner stalk a lion put elephant tusks on the wall..

Mention the word hallucination and they are shaking in their boots. Shitting their pants ...

Nothing terrifies them more in their brain's arithmetic than a confrontation with the unconscious. They will run around the prickly pear at 5 in the morning but they will not flag down their own selfhood for a look under the hood, at what makes the pistons go round.

Politicians with Business and Law degrees exercise their will to power because of psychological deficiencies. They need an ego decked out in extrinsic lore. They need people to tyrannize to believe they got it together. We are led by mental midgets, intellectually and morally bankrupt. They grabbed the microphone because they were paranoid without it.

THE YOUNG AND THE DISLOCATED

As mentioned, I have a schizophrenic friend who used, unwittingly, divergent thinking to stay afloat when he was young. The dislocation can be strenuous as in the heretofore mentioned Multiple Personality disorder where rigid boundaries are constructed in the neurology.

It's a good strategy for a psychology to handle abuse and trauma. It's a most unfortunate way to grow up. In a very real sense we all grow up, the different parts of our anatomy pledged to different game plans. We lose touch with our toes and fingers which we avoided intimate contact. The physical body and the emotional body are battling it out on a daily basis.

Awareness unscrambles signals. To never give it any thought is to reach the end without your house in order. For most the mind is a contraption, with a modus operandi, fallen into place over time. That contraption will hold you hostage.

Simpletons rule the world. People who graft to certain motifs in corporations are killing the human notion of transcendence and evolution. We are a statistic.

Kings and Little Ones

By perpetuating myths of masculinity males inhibit empathy.

This is the sweat in the sports locker room that makes the toughest toe the line. If Ray Lewis has the dressing room he is the boss.

Who has the locker room and what does that entail when professional athletes have to unquestioningly confront injustice? If you are a team player the team is everything and you are nothing. Simply being there is a kind of verbal hazing.

That's as good as it gets. There are a lot of big boys demanding that the universal mentality of athletes prevail against any softening, that they remain hard core and dumbass. Knuckleheads.

I've been in the lacrosse, football, baseball, and hockey locker rooms. I guarantee you the intellectual ceiling is pretty low. Try to engage a professional athlete in an intellectual conversation and you will fail. And you can alienate the locker room.

The most ridiculous shows involve live sound -bites from the football field. Most of these guys have grade 4 reading ability their vocabulary 200 words.

Everything is conducted from the mapping of frequent flyer routes that offer up revolving door manifestos and colloquial herd-speak. Athletes stick together.

Pauli sees the physics of light and dark as integral to psychic forces. Darkness is ignorance.

Darkness is the prescriptive nature of science and its limited 'blind' grasp.

Science inhibits breakthrough. Kuhn points out that those who colour outside the lines are the breakthrough scientists, artists of new canvases.

Keeping the finger on the pulse of creativity is the most challenging thing for any scientist or artist or human being.

The imagination is a hard road to hoe. For Pauli and anyone who explores it, the fluidity of image and thoughts provoked in the imagination, reveals territory often shrouded in ambiguity. One thing is partially embodied by several causalities. Confluence upon confluence. In the 100 billion neuron universe a single neuron can hook to hundreds of active relationships. One's connection is as fluid as one's moods and thoughts. To open the creativity portal you need to be willing to be re-enlightened daily. Most painters don't want to face the uncertainty that the imagination offers.

Normal Science sees active imagination as heresy. The tendency is always to play it safe, lean towards the rational, the arithmetic (STEM) of being. The self you 'think' of as your self is a portrait of a lot of assumptions crystallizing into an image that will prevent other selves from emerging.

The problem is those individuated selves that are more authentic are absolutely necessary.

By the time one gets through school it's difficult to think outside the box. This is the forgone conclusion. This is precisely why the human mind is teetering on the abyss. We have become numb, comfortably numb, and the rug is being pulled out from under us. And we demand that reality be the way we understand it.

plastic fantastic LSD Trips

We were out on the 5th line, outside of my home town, Orangeville. It was summer. We were still teenagers or close to it.

We were camping out overnight in the summer on hills which would be lined with skiers in winter. It was called Valley Schuss.

The campsite overlooked the Hockley Valley, the same Hockley Valley where James Cameron would go on family drives when he was little. James' cousin lived next door to my brother and his grandmother lived near Alton.

Hockley was a name he remembered when it came to making the *Titanic*. He would use it for a character.

Neurogenesis

We my friend and the 2 girls we would be divorced from re: the Christmas Eve fire in the bush. We had taken LSD at 9 pm or so. We had a campfire and I decided to test how far I could carry the warmth in my body down the steep hill. I was thinking of a poem called the 'Church of Fear' I was working on. About 2 am there is a car's headlights and sound going through the winding Hockley Road.

It was weird watching the lights from such a height.

Then BOOM a collision. Then silence. We had no idea what sort of collision.

We had no choice. We jumped in the Dodge Dart.

When we came around a sharp bend between the 5th and 6th line, there was a figure, a man, in the middle of the road. It was like something out of a nightmare. There was no car in sight.

Just a single human being, a man. Seeing this apparition emerge into the car's headlights caused me some distress. I let out a horrified scream I would have a hard time living down.

The young guy was bleeding from the forehead. He was wet. His shoulder was somewhat exposed. His car had ended up upside down in the Hockley River, or so we local yokels called it. It was really the Nottawasaga. The accident, we couldn't really attend to. This was a minimalist effort. If he was dying we needed to help. But one didn't feel confident to negotiate reality in that context. As extraordinary as my LSD trips were they don't come close to those of Marc Lewis the neuroscientist who talks about the addicted brain.

Neuroscientist Marc Lewis, author of, *Memoirs of an Addicted Brain*, describes his LSD trips very profoundly. The stuff I did on LSD comes nowhere close to this addict turned neuroscientist reporting on his experience. I can literally feel LSD when I read his account. Lewis' book is one of the best books I've ever read. It reads like Catcher in The Rye meets the Grateful Dead. It's a thriller. It does not read like a book on neuroscience by a neuroscientist.

The mysterious man in the middle of the road, all wet and bleeding and with a noticeable slight arm injury was a schoolmate who had left his friend's stag. Though we didn't ask him, it's probably safe to assume he had been drinking.

His friend was marrying an old girlfriend of mine. On the way to the hospital I looked at his bloodied forehead. Blood seemed to be coming out but also going back in. How bad was he hurt? We didn't know. He was talking like someone okay, not concussed or anything.

We dropped him at Emerge in Orangeville, at the very hospital where I was born, not wanting any encounters with the establishment.

Decades later, at a high school reunion that same guy--- hadn't seen him in 40 years... maintained he had been dropped off back at the Highlands where the stag was going on. Weird!

Acapulco Gold

A girlfriend and I were in the inertia of a break-up when we went to Acapulco. I had taken a couple window pane LSD with me and was determined to take it on the Acapulco Beach during the day. I would never do LSD at night in a foreign country.

I was a little reckless at the time. When a relationship goes up in flames it's not easy. This girl was half my age and I had gone out on a limb for her. Now the limb was being cut off.

One day I did the LSD, or we did. I rented a catamaran only having once experimented with one in the Bahamas a couple years previous. I had a grand total of 30 minutes sailing experience. In the Bahamas it wasn't the same girlfriend.

I wanted my partner to go topless like a playboy video featuring playmate Barbara Edwards. Yes I was that kind of guy. I'm glad I grew up.

First I had to get past the people. We got out of view of our hotel fairly quickly and indeed we got beyond the coast of Resort hotels. We barely could see land. Total absolute foolery.

It never occurred to me that we might not make it back. As it turned out we were burnt like lobsters but we made it back. That pink ball in the sky, the Acapulco sun, was unrelenting. We were primitives in a primitive situation. LSD can zero in on neurodynamics making every experience one experience.

Relationships of mine look different in the rear-view mirror. Lust and love can get wrapped up in each other. Termination can be painful. After this failed relationship I would go on a two-year walkabout—no dating. I had to learn how to live with myself. I had to have everything uncertain.

"Entropy is a dimensionless quantity that is used for measuring uncertainty about the state of a system but it can also imply physical qualities, where high entropy is synonymous with high disorder. Entropy is applied here in the context of states of consciousness and their associated neurodynamics, with a particular focus on the psychedelic state. The psychedelic state is considered an exemplar of a primitive or primary state of consciousness that preceded the development of modern, adult, human, normal waking consciousness," (The Entropic Brain: a theory of conscious states informed by

neuroimaging research with psychedelic drugs, p. 1).

Neurodynamics is what we are all about. Neurodynamics shape the mind.

Neurodynamics is akin to what Carlos Castenada called the Assemblage Point. Shift the neurodynamics and the Assembly Point shifts.

I was one with the experience during the sailing adventure never questioning anything. It was primitive. It was nature. LSD can give you a special place in your own mythology, a pivotal place, between sky and water, between life and death. There is only one spot one gap between life and death--- and that is now.

When searching for a higher order the bargaining has to be in good faith. You can't con transcendence. By seeing the brain as primitively enthralled with 'uncertainty' and 'high disorder' is, of course, the very character of entropy. This I suggest is the chaos that can be triggered when the old self dies and dissolves even as the new self is being 'born' again. After uncertainty comes new certainty - a born again certainty.

This is why epiphany is a fairly frequent thing with psychedelics. This is why bad habits can be broken.

In Eliot's *Journey of Magi* are the words:

**Birth or Death? There was a birth certainly,
  We had evidence and no doubt.
I had seen birth and death,
But had thought they were different   (Selected Poetry, p. 98)**

Eliot talks about the bitter agony of death and new birth. When something 'big' dies in your daily relationship with yourself it is a 'big' deal. After my marital separation and any relationship breakup, I went around with a great weight on me. Now and again that weight wouldn't be there. The levity was physical and mental. An old relationship dies, goes up in flames, and like a phoenix you have to re-originate.

STRANGER IN A STRANGE LAND

More horrific was the thought of returning to the people--- the unexperienced and unborn to live **"in the old dispensation, with an alien people clutching their gods."**

Once you've tasted enlightenment the old way can seem tedious and unnecessary. What is at the crux here is the need to pass oneself off as a card carrying member of the tribe. The old dispensation is Normalization.

The defining feature of 'primary states' is elevated entropy. Before filing cabinets and data processors there was necessarily unfiled, uncatalogued, unlabelled reality. This primitive place is pre-mathematics and pre-language. I do believe that the state is a psychic journey and the self we carry into a primitive state, is an unconscious self, not void of individuation.

This primary state is the appeal of Ayahuasca, especially if contextually one is in the Amazon forest.

But that's not all that goes on with a trip. That's precisely where Pauli and Jung come in. By navigating the necessary psychiatry of the self as individual, a return to primal force, enlivens the archetype. Your personal givings and misgivings make it all ultra-personal and profound. Challenge of standing one's ground is archetypically necessary. It's the perilous journey. Its Kierkegaard's leap of faith and it's the tightrope over the abyss. It's you as bridge between here and now.

GO ASK ALICE WHEN SHE'S TEN FEET TALL

Falling down the rabbit hole cascades into total uncertainty, about everything. There is nothing to grab onto. But Alice had a good time. LSD can be a good time.

Everything inside and out is shifting gears -- size, speed, up and down. The essential thing is: nothing is the same.

When one embraces the unknowable one lowers the subconscious need to know. With a relaxed new 'psyche'-confronted version of self, the unknowable loses its threat. Just like that divergence becomes a friend.

There is no proof against the idea that dissipative energy is something that is of essence unrecyclable or recyclable.

It does make elegant sense. The energy dissipating during a car rusting or a glass shattering are dissipating energies, slow and fast. Where does energy go when stuff falls apart? We plug into it and it becomes creative flow. What could be more beautiful than the universe recycling itself through the human mind?

Meanwhile back at the ranch the white picket fence and the rose garden and the whole kit and caboodle are values of a history disappearing in the rear-view mirror. A new tomorrow is dawning. What on Earth are we going to do when escalating global tension and Normalization turns us into madmen?

As likely as not, entropy is a magnetic slipstream, a zero point conjunction. When everything is torn down and nothing rebuilt the material reality is ungrounded. Matter is in an unknown sublimated state, as a place in between, in between matter and energy. It is space easily induced by psychoid reactions.

The reason it is susceptible to psychoid infusion is because of the immateriality of it all. Dark matter, dark flow and dark energy are part and parcel of this. Entropy is very likely DARK FLOW.

When your prescriptive lock-step grip on the past relaxes, the step into the void re-characterizes the self. The self, having nowhere to go within plasticity opens in desperation a portal to Entropy. The porthole exists in Neurogenesis. Actually depending on the ratio of alteration one can say one re-constitutes.

This re-constitution is explored somewhat in the movie Altered States with William Hurt. The unconscious recognizes that you want to do business—you don't need any more small talk. Indeed small talk is a blockage in the mind and entropy is lightyears bigger than that.

Entropy has no allegiance to fore or aft. It is outside the sequential viability of axiomatic things. Zero energy has been written about as a source of instantaneous exponentially. This makes 'absolute' sense.

Absolutes as states of being aroused the interest of Soren Kierkegaard. He talked about the absolute relationship to the absolute. In an absolute relationship to the absolute the knight of good faith leaps the abyss of human normalization and rescues the self.

We are talking about entropic accelerants when we talk psychedelics.

Of course people can't go around stoned on drugs. This is my point. We've characterized drugs because of Reefer Madness and microwaved babies and positioned ourselves historically. Because of this error in judgement fostered by white males afraid of their own unconscious monsters, we pay a price. Re-constitutive forces that could save us, we are afraid of. . The elixir, the quickening, is as miraculous and as elemental (alchemical) as folklore gets, as archetypal as the spectral continuum reflects. And beautifully it launches with little fanfare, with the most casual and ambiguous stimulus. It is not the property of Kings and Queens and CEOs. It is standard in every human brain.

And it is accelerated during the psychedelic experience.

Re-constitution is about re-birth and re-incarnating a conscious presence in the valuation process, in seeing each moment of brain plasticity as a plus or minus event.

Think of psychic energy. What is the nature of mind itself? Tesla said everything comes down to energy, vibration and frequency. Certainly the mind in co-ordinating itself in space, like all space, has a quantum reality to it. How could it not? How could it me matter of a different sort, a matter existing outside space.

It is not the primitive expression as in pre-conscious humans that a psychedelic experience brings about. It is like Pauli and Jung's psychic confrontation with the unconscious.

The Pauli brain is not a static brain. Static psychic electricity triggers Alzheimer's. Pauli's brain is a growing brain, growing through levels of awareness in an individuation process. For Pauli and Jung, unaware of neurogenesis, the compass was attached to specifying structures like anima, animus and synchronicity. We, unlike all humans before us, can stand on the shoulders of plasticity knowing change is scientifically possible. Plasticity can be created and destroyed. Synaptic potentiation can be aroused. Alternately and more prevalently axons and dendrites can shrivel up.

Picasso was impressed by primitive art and it influenced him greatly. Apollinaire stole an ancient African Bust from the Louvre for Picasso.

Picasso was able to experiment creatively with tapping into his own primitive core. I don't believe this is so pure as to dismiss plasticity overlays in the previous temporal self the already in process, individuated self. Picasso was Picasso.

The chance equipment of the hour is the equipment you build in the brain. When called upon you have it. Like a Swiss Army knife it is there when you need it. For Wordsworth and Coleridge you carry a threshold of awareness that can be born and materialize at any moment. Cannabis users can set up an internal space dedicated to this threshold. Drugs or no drugs, everyone should strive to modify their chance equipment of the hour.

Picasso's primitive expressionism was contoured to his own psyche, to his own psychology, and particularly in his case, around the centerpiece of women. His best friend and sister died young. His girlfriend died young. Important women raked Picasso over the coals and the friction became primitive. That is what is primitive about it, striking a connection that is authentic and 'newborn'. For the self, the symbolism is real and strikes a chord. Our enabling personal bubble, what Jung calls persona creates a synthesis of form and volume implicated in the symbolic interactionism. We are symbolized. Face recognition software can even calculate whether we are happy or not.

The Lost Chord

"The relinquishment of 'ego' enables profound existential or 'peak' experiences to occur that could have a lasting positive impact on behaviour and outlook …. Innumerable cases of apparent spontaneous insights about 'self' or 'nature' exist in the literature on psychedelics," (The Entropic Brain: a theory of conscious states informed by neuroimaging research with psychedelic drugs, p.

In an entropic leap of faith the world is evolved, re-ordered and to some degree reconstituted in the essence of transformative dimensionality. Transformative spontaneity is neurogenesis.

The ego is of course a construct of our thought, mostly using Freud's ideas. I see Freud to Jung like I see Newtonian Science to Einstein Science. One includes the other. The libido is Freud's idea of the sex drive. For Jung it is much more complicated involving layers of layers of anima and animus issues. For Jung and Pauli having your house in order internally was important than owning a chalet in St. Moritz.

Kris Kristofferson said, although I'm recalling from memory, **'Freedom is just another word for nothing left to lose.'**

Relinquishment is very Indian mystic and Buddhist and Hindu. Christian society doesn't respect that Christ too had nothing.

Part of the transformative power comes from soulful and psychological alignment in the individuation process. **Spontaneous insights happen when the mind is cultivated for insight.**

"A mature ego endows the mind with a capacity for metacognition i.e. an ability to reflect on one's own thoughts and behaviours," (The Entropic Brain, p.9).

Depending on your degree of normalization you value this or that thought. You favour it by thinking it over thinking something else.

With such awareness moving forward one can set up a romance with resonance factors that induce awareness.

Reflection is a capacitation process. Your chance equipment of the hour modifies and evolves. You learn how to handle chance. You learn how to be lost. Divergence and Discontinuity are inspiring and liberating. You become a child of the universe; your parents like Jesus' parents a necessary causality nothing more.

This is Biblical. Lose the self (ego) to find the self. The mind has facilitated the daily agenda and ordered your reality. When this event horizon powers down, the lights go out in Bangkok (*can make a hard man humble*) and you can't see what normally fills your head. This causes panic.

The eternal is exposed to your vision. Needless to say this is discombobulating. It disenfranchises everything that your franchises have been marketing for years, within your personal image-making machinery. The most frequent experience on psychedelics is the most disconcerting. People feel like a fraud, like they are living a lie. The lie is Normalization.

In the starkest backdrop imaginable you are facing off with an elusive you and you stand intermittently and simultaneously on both sides of the self. This contrived self is weighed in the balance, and found wanting. The contrived self is the 'ego'.

When any veil is ripped away or any shining light knocks you off your donkey, the world that comes into view is a different world. Your place in that world is magically altered.

This is unmistakable and a theme that ran through the early Timothy Leary LSD experiments with prisoners to divinity students. You can see the light and have revelation revealed.

Fact sheets were there.

Timothy Leary, before his death, made an audio tape that was about brain plasticity. He was no fool. When he said,' Tune in, Turn on and Drop Out,' he knew Normalization had hacked our culture. He knew Normalization would reach a crescendo, an apex, and hell would break loose.

You can bring order to it but not with the facilitation measuring sticks once deemed appropriate now simply lack the measure. They are useless tools. The finite world is awash with pictures and thoughts, and metaphors and imaginings. This new mind transcends the embedded former self. The new self merges with a profoundly resonating substance of a different quality, a different physics. It becomes 'substantial' hence material within the self and knowing this self, more and more, is the quest.

I WANT MY MAYPO

Maypo was a cereal advertised on American TV. I remember it like this: A kid in a high chair would pound his fists up and down and cry out: I want my Maypo. His uncle would shove a big spoon of Maypo in his mouth. He would swallow it and his face would light up with a big smile.

What's in your wallet?

Everyone has a Maypo; it might be football or flying an airplane or wanting what you want when you want it. Want controls and defines us like little else. Want defined Sampson and it was his undoing. This is the lesson you don't want. You don't want to be dragged through the mud just because you couldn't put the brakes on your desire. The culprit is not the emotions but the lack of evolution.

Everything is a drug inside your body. Chocolate, coffee, grapefruit all break down into biochemistry. Love is a drug.

If entropy suppression furnishes normal waking consciousness with a constrained quality it is because co-ordinates of experience continuously ratify the contract with self. Maturation in a sub-critical mode happens. You fall into place.

All humans go through the daily grind ignoring consciousness. Their metabolism and biochemistry become established.

Such constraint reflects the social embeddedness of the individual and the radius of the understanding that, the individual is privy too. Uneducated white Americans are Trump's strongest supporters because the radius of their learning, brackets their perception.

To me, LSD can invoke a completely primitive state of mind, no holds barred, but that is the triumph of the moment outside normal plasticity. That is the leverage of zero when you power down the day-to-day mind structure. Something has to power up. In the moment one is left in the lurch, there will necessarily be a psychological infusion that comes from learned negotiation with the self. Adjusting our thinking is perpetual regardless of whether we change or re-establish what is there. Neurogenesis can make transformation immediate and long-lasting.

That's what the higher critical state tries to resolve. Arithmetic, language, imagination, empathy are featured in balance with one another. The networking through the corpus callosum refracts powerfully into all brain regions. When the whole orchestra fires up, we are attending the complex brain in all its richness.

The function enhanced by the plasticity activated psychedelic brain means a lot is up for grabs, contrasted with the daily terrain where habit buries the self in typical correlatives.

Profound change is possible. One can negotiate on a new level where divergence exists.

I mention my LSD trips because the literature is scant when it comes to the sort of self-experimenting stuff I did. Particularly, what has been written up often involves clinical settings. The day the world went black at the Orangeville reservoir is not in my memory, except for that moment. Memories that incite riot in us are deeply etched. Moments on LSD have a special place.

To make a huge deal of it is to overplay the cautionary tale.

David Stewart of the Eurythmics did LSD every day or two for a long time. LSD does not fry your brain. It doesn't curl your dendrites like an Afro.

To mix it up with cocaine and heroin is an error. Cocaine and heroin fire and wire the brain like a forest fire leaving behind charred and bedraggled bushes and trees.

THE CRYSTAL CAVE

Neurogenesis and neuroplasticity are on line during a psychedelic drug experience. Like Merlin reflecting on the future through the prismatic mingling of crystal projection, the mind by way of image and hallucination becomes forthright in its task orientation. Hallucination trajectories often reflect the nature of one's needs to scale different subconscious and unconscious experience. The constructs within the mirror neurons themselves oscillate the time passage into non-incremental, un-boundary-ied explorative accounts. These are shapes in our consciousness morphing us favourably.

Of course we are systemic in our default modalities. We hold ourselves together this way. We jump through the hoops of the system. We measure ourselves the way others measure us. We get a pat on the back or a frown. Our future is calculated. By mirroring complex concocted visions we can sort out what is likely to happen if we keep on keeping on. On psychedelics the mind is on the mission of its life.

It's all mission statement. It all counts.

Each generation is inheriting mind constructs designed to favour the Autism end of the spectrum. This means decreasing the attention span by fixation with sequencing. This fosters a diminishing of inter-subjectivity and individuation particularly, and most crucially, involving a lessening of inter-subjectivity resolution. WE forget how to be human. A lack of inter-subjectivity resolution is the direct source of the biggest problem facing humanity. It is why people go postal. It's why every day of the week can offer up a new crisis of self-determination in people who are alienated and alone.

In many ways the most accentuated attention that History has given to consciousness (since the Greeks 500 BC) was with the English Romantic poets. They delved into mind. Outlined in books concerning the influence of opium on the imagination, ideas surface about the nature of mind. See Opium and The Romantic Imagination by Alethea Hayter. Baudelaire in France was likewise interested in these special mental events particularly 'visions'..

Drug addiction plagued both De Quincey and Coleridge. Even in the statelier Poet Laureate Wordsworth the imagination was focal point when he poeticized. Elusive spots in time could be navigated only if one could access a spontaneous outpouring of powerful emotions. The hole in the wall is a wormhole in time, a time to absorb time, time without boundary.

Eternity in an hour is a wormhole moment. Infinity in a grain of sand is how Blake put it. **When you are in that moment it is a type of suspended animation outside of time.**

Time and space dilation, intuited, imagined and actual.

An LSD trip puts the tripper outside of time like in the movie *Easy Rider*. The graveyard is a place where one feels 'time'. One can breathe the analogy of feeling time. "I've got an idea, let's go outside."

Similarly creativity unleashed, sets the stage for metaphoric reality and metaphorical ascendency. Metaphorical ascendancy is the nature of the mission towards complexity. Psychological triumph is very much possible when interactions maintain symbolism quanta in the unconscious. Like Odysseus tied to the mast we get to hear the song of the Sirens and live to tell the tale.

By perching himself above Tintern Abby, Wordsworth could unwind his youth like a movie. You can see mistakes and triumphs of the soul from a different angle. You can see time and make time see you. I made the pilgrimage to the Lake District and Wordsworth's cottage in 1980. We took a rowboat out on the famous Lake Windermere. I had Wordsworth's great-great-grand-niece sign a book on the Lake District for me. It's beautiful to walk through the ancient gate knowing Wordsworth knew that gate intimately.

Once in a deeply reflective mood, riding a horse in the Prelude, Wordsworth's glance bounces off the reflex of a star into an experiential metaphorical exploration. This is a profound and exemplary description of metaphor in action, growing, taking shape in real time—in process of happening. It was Wordsworth who said in 1802, 1802 for God's sake, that 'the world is too much with us, its coming and going.' For Wordsworth, getting out of time was the equivalent of accessing eternity. It makes sense that Schnabel's movie of Van Gogh is entitled *At Eternity's Gate*. Vincent transformed his life in his canvases. Creativity accesses neurogenesis which opens up the eternal flow of entropy. Time and Space don't count. Where you go is some eternal moment. When you come back you are replenished. Vincent after shooting himself spent his last day calm, smoking his pipe, conversing with

Theo. Vincent would never know how famous he would become, how valued.

If you can access with the chance equipment of the hour, a spontaneous overflow of powerful feeling you are ready. You can touch the magic and put your finger on the pulse. If you can be smitten by a thousand daffodils, you have your mojo working. This reflects an escape route for thoughts and imaginings. You are your own conjuring. Your plasticity will carry the day for better or for worse. There is no getting around it.

Direct observation is never possible. We filter it through our bubble of understanding with the equipment of the conscious self. We are looking at 'self' with the machinery of self and we superimpose that idea conceptually. From this notion: mind as clock or computer we compute reality. We derive different information because of how we think, we think. We tag information coming in, according to what we think, we are thinking, when we aren't even paying attention. And then we hand this pre-packaged, pre-digested, information construct to the next generation.

Albert Einstein said, "Reality is merely an illusion, albeit a very persistent one."

I shall say it again. The things we need reminding of we need to keep within range.

By being defensive about our own thoughts we are incorporating the illusion allowing this persistence to persist. Wilhelm Reich maps this territory very insightfully with his character armour theory. Character armour for all its power is an illusion that can break down in the archetypal setting of the psychedelic arena. Jane Fonda talks about her character armour and how it eventually was sucking the life out of her.

Once on LSD I was gathering myself in the mirror. My face started to morph into other faces, then older and older versions of my own face. My hair thinned and went white. Eventually the skin transitioned off my face and I looked at my own skeleton. The vision acquiesced in me and didn't freak me out. It was like a straight forward explanation of archetypal life cycle, and hence non-threatening. I felt like the wise old man. This is 'keeper' knowledge stuff, not unlike other deep insights afforded by psychedelic experience that map out the life cycle.

In the novel *White Oleander* the main character does acid with a friend who tells her not to look in the mirror. The acid trip in *White Oleander* moves to a gallery and the drug opens up art in a special way.

"Some of the paintings opened up, like windows, like doors …. I could reach into Cézanne's peaches and cherries …. I felt I could have painted all the paintings myself. The acid kept coming on and coming on, I didn't know how much higher I could get …. This was higher than high. Two-hundredth floor, five- hundredth floor,

Van Gogh's night sky,' (Janet Fitch, White Oleander, p. 276).

The connection between psychedelic vision and art is a profound one. Dali and his wife Gala did acid. But so did Steve Jobs and half of Silicon Valley. As humans we have one imagination. For sure Edison and Henry Ford could be characterized as imaginative and creative. I say, there is a difference. Like Daniel Tammet they are on the spectrum. Amazing things link up but it is gadgetry.

Psychiatry and psychology are not considered hard science and could never pass the litmus test of rigid science. Psychology is everywhere apparent self-evidentiary stuff. Science censors the ramifications of psychology because ironically of where they are positioned psychologically on the spectrum.

 Science is simply slow on the draw

 or maybe they believe they don't have brains, or minds

    Or complexes or perceptual limits,

    or frightening moments or

    Poetry hanging on the lips

    or colossal doubt

Including a fetish for the measureable and tangible.

We have to recognize what comes with the territory of being human, what it means to have a hundred billion neuron universe attached to our shoulders.

Scientists like Amit Goswami (*Quantum Healing, The Self-Aware Universe*) are outsiders.

This is a fateful error, ingrained into social structure, sign of the times stuff. Continental drift was ridiculed as pure fantasy when first tabled as an idea. Relativity was seen by many as Jewish Science. There are books on how rigidly sanctimonious is the Science establishment and how clueless it is in conceptual overhaul aspects.

Truth isn't truth unless it is popularized in the collective mind. The litmus is no litmus at all. Give the monkeys a banana or a beer for a buck and they'll vote for you. That's the wave-length of thought processes. Many people can't see through obvious ploys. Currently the chief cause of death in the UK for males under 50 is suicide. Maybe I said this already. The male, because of male ideation, has nowhere to go in the future and they crack up.. Some of broken males are the true leaders in perception. Guys like Darryl Strawberry gutted by depression re-constitute as a new person. The male-male is going back where barbarism is a philosophy they can grapple with and behaviourism they can understand. Aping each other at the end of time.

Indeed, walk into a Scientist's household and you'll see the same cross section of medication as in any household.

We are all inundated with the same mortal coil landscape and consequences are real.

Our society believes implicitly in these 'universal' pharmaceutical drugs despite a lack of understanding of long term side effects. Universal acceptance is assumption normalization gone viral. Most of the positive effects of anti-depressants are equalled by placebo effect yet the side-effects are serious, often leading to other medical conditions. Young people hooked early, frequently have a sad future ahead. With the stamp of approval of the accepted way of doing business in this world, the fired and wired memory, the held fast illusion of reality is fortified and un-transgress-able. Preferences become social and psychological without the metacognition capacity to separate drive and ambition from insightful research.

We worship pharmacy. It's a prescription for disaster.

BEDSIDE MANNER

A frequently televised documentary on Super Humans had a sequence where an arctic runner known for barefoot runs across the ice was placed in a bathtub of ice to measure how he controlled his body temperature. With him was a lab coat scientist with his menacing measuring apparatus writing down information. That the vibes in this situation are entirely contradistinctive to the freedom of this individual's normal experience wasn't considered. For a human being to presume on another, as Eliot would say, is a transgression of deep significance. This is why Hamlet resents Rosencrantz and Guildenstern, because they try to play him like a flute, spying as they are for the King.

Nobody likes to be a lab rat, poked and prodded and measured. The moment that human-to-human connection isn't there, meaning putting oneself in the shoes of the other, everything human can go haywire. The experiment always becomes a psychological event. Science wants to move things into a bracketed reality. It's happiest when it murders to dissect.

In the end, the experience in the bathtub is not relative to understanding his capacity to run barefoot across an icy expanse, with the sun and the atmosphere of nature. What they proved is simply that a lab technician treating a human as a monkey is 'subconsciously' upsetting for the monkey. This is precisely an anecdote as to how Science misses the boat when reducing everything to simplified equations. Their cookie cutter approach lops off the edges. It turns a human being into a thinking slab of meat.

Marcus Welby

Marcus Welby inspired such confidence as a TV doctor he received tons of requests from people want his diagnosis. Only now in this very second do I see the subliminal connection in the name Well Be. .Many studies confirm a profound placebo effect accompanies a doctor's efforts if the patient thinks the doctor truly cares. Caring goes into the mirror neurons, creating a picture of a healthy outcome.

How the office is set up is important. Is it warm and inviting? Is it harsh with rudimentary, barely human, interaction? Many doctors arriving in the profession are assembly line doctors. They lack empathy and bedside manner. These are no longer taught.

The equations are not relative at all outside certain contexts yet Science strives to function everywhere with the same apparatus, the same experiment designs. For Science one-size fits all. That a scientist could be that lacking in self-awareness seems remarkable till we look at the spectrum. Science relies on detaching the self from being human. It has its place on the spectrum—low inter-subjectivity and metaphorical grasp.

Even this scientist, if the next day went to see a heart specialist in a white lab coat, would feel the consequence of those archetypal vibes. **By archetype I mean the hero to villain spectrum, the innocence to experience spectrum, and the symbolization of representational forces. Interactive symbolism goes a long way to create climate and atmosphere and it behooves one to set up experiments with this in mind.**

Psychedelics are seen as a joke, a triviality by many scientists. This is too bad.

The potentiality for creative divergent thinking is inherent in the psychedelic experience.

Divergent thinking creates a breeding ground for creative spontaneity. Everybody is creative,

This is to say we have a place in the brain for creative endeavour that psychedelics orchestrate with urgency and divergence. Psychedelics reveal what goes on in everyday brains facing a dissociation or divergence crisis. Divergence happens as we age if we wander away from our maturational settling. It makes sense to sample divergence before it samples you. Divergence can be threatening. A familiarity with it is the best medicine.

Disorganize the typical brain strategies that we face off with everyday occurrence and you encounter the birth of the new. Of course it is dangerous, but more dangerous in some individuals for whom self-realization is the most distant of prospects.

The great disorganizer drug can reveal ugly truths from behind the daily masquerade and the typical façade. You can catch a glimpse in the mirror you don't like. It can fracture you. It is primal in how it reverts to an unconscious encounter, not organized by prevailing social themes and trends.

There is a transcending organizing principle no longer satisfied with proclamation by habit. Consciousness strives for complexity. We in our short-sightedness unleash an executive decision that overrules complexity supplanting it with the habitual.

The cognition of primal man is less organized, more synesthesia-oriented. Mirror neurons with their motor mechanisms fused directly to experience establish the surreal as a commentary on reality and illusion. Beyond the real is the new real, a real more truthful for not being compromised by pleasant valley Sunday infantilism.

FLOAT LIKE A BUTTERFLY

Mohamed Ali, as I've often quoted elsewhere, says a man who thinks the same way at 50 as he did at 20 has wasted 30 years of his life.

We have to take growth seriously or the species is doomed. Most men don't think that way. They still tell the same audience the same jokes. On LSD your whole narrative becomes a movie that you are inside of. Reflectability is everywhere. Rocks breathe. Trees breathe. When you move, you see body trails, a flow of colours, like time lapse photography. Everything is endowed with more sensibility. "The room swirled with color and motion," (Janet Fitch, White Oleander, p. 379).

The point is the interest level is there. Athletes and male ideation advocates could actually find psychedelics vitally interesting. Task focus shifts. Brain action moves left to right brain. The big picture and the big plan show different avenues of living, that open sesame.

This comes on like a dream. All your certainties heretofore were lockstep with your habituated ways of seeing. This is very different The psychology of perception studies, reveal your vista as controlled by your psyche. Here in this psychedelic realm uncertainty is freedom. If nothing is certain then filling in the blanks is a more challenging proposition. You have to make stuff up not fake stuff up. Making stuff up, gaps into reciprocity energy which is **entropic** and can take you anywhere in the never-been. The never-been is infinite.

Two things are going on in a truly expansive creative event. One involves dissolution of habit. This cleanses the doors of perception of build-up and built in biases, biochemically enshrined.

Destructuring is disorientation. The ego is under attack.

This can itself can be profoundly dismantling. Goswami echoes the earlier thought**, "It takes a strong ego to handle the destructuring of the old that makes room for the new,"** (The Self-Aware Universe, p.226).

The structure of axons and dendrites don't physically move forward. They are torn down in the sense they are no longer used. Symbolically they have stepped aside as firing and wiring speeds to a new resonance. To self-realize, in an existentially satisfying way, is an experience deeper than happiness. Happiness comes and goes without you losing resolve. You discover that your mind is your way out. You can navigate destructuring and restructuring. One remembers necessarily that small incremental or particle steps are simultaneously 'wave' constituents. The whole organism marches to the finite and the infinite. Like those flocks of thousands of birds who gyrate as if one body, the personality takes on and dismisses shape. The psychokinetic reality of indigenous shape-shifting is representative of a personal dimensionality.

Movement has a psychokinetic intent. It need not be a discipline, simply a subconscious rendering. You can pretend you are doing Tai Chi and invent similar movements. On psychedelics you can feel yourself inside yourself inside a body. Alexander Technique, Meir Schneider, and Carlos Castaneda feature 'pure' understandings of the body.

Creative endeavour fulfills this notion of the unexplored and reconnects us to the mortal coil.

Implicit, not explicit, ambiguous, not definitive…intuitive not logical.

My wife had a recent workshop on the blue eyes, brown eyes experiment. Replicated a thousand times it tells us intelligence is managed and governed by expectations. Bloomers bloom when they think they are smart and are treated as smart. Science still wants hard fact based intelligence, which of course, is as erroneous as can be. But it suits their hierarchy, their formula. It's entrenched to think there are smart people and stupid people. Bloomers bloom when enriched plasticity blooms.

The trouble with science is how square it is...how far behind the times. How when it gets on the dancefloor, it gets dizzy and has to find a chair.

That's precisely the danger as manifest in America and elsewhere, where ignorance packages people in the bleakest reality, rendering their plasticity inaccessible and non-educable. They can't budge an inch on the spectrum. Muscle heads and cowboys prefer not to think of any salvation. Their salvation is with the crowd, their palms holding a beer. They don't envisage the High Noon day of judgement, where without friends, Jesus weighs them in the balance, holds their lives up to the light.

This is what Saul felt when he saw the light. This is the same guy as Saint Paul, the real rock on which Christianity is built. Paul went 180 degrees from persecutor of Christians to the guy who would write the letters, constituting the very fabric of the Christian belief. If Peter was the Rock Paul was the press agent.

What Pauli did on his symbolic road to Damascus is not something that appeals to your science geek or tech head. Psychiatry hasn't dawned on them. Jung and Freud are as distant as John the Baptist or Beowulf.

Neuroplasticity and Neurogenesis reflect, directly and literally, a kind of salvation. We can change. Imagine what that means in the short run and the long run. The best way to access neurogenesis is via creativity. I continuously surprise myself and that is the most ingratiating life-affirming thing about art. Even God is known to have dabbled in creation.

VISUAL VERBAL BRIDGING BRAMALEA SECONDARY

As a teacher I designed a video arts course with super 8 filmmaking, photography, and advertising including making up ads and filming them. It was a precursor of media literacy with a strong creative component. In this course we would read a story like *Rocking Horse Winner*. I'd have students write a description of how it could be filmed...establishing shots close-ups, etc. Then we would watch the TVO archives film and compare notes. We'd read the scene in Dickey's *Deliverance* before and after the deer incident. We'd direct it according to our creativity. Then we'd watch the movie. This sifting back and forth helps in several ways to structure the mind with words and pictures.

We'd talk about this ability to visualize and animate...how we can improve reading verbal cues, so as to amplify scenes in our minds. Visual verbal bridging is particularly important if people are trying to animate their own imaginations in the act of reading. An image like Holden Caulfield standing above the football field knowing he is digesting the scene for the very last time can burn deep in the mind plate.

"Anyway, I kept standing next to that crazy cannon, looking down at the games and freezing my ass off. Only, I wasn't watching the game too

much. What I was really hanging around for was, I was trying to feel some kind of a goodbye. I mean I've left schools in places I didn't even know I was leaving them. I hate that. I don't care if it's a sad goodbye or a bad goodbye, but when I leave a place I like to *know* I'm leaving it. If you don't, you feel even worse," (J.D. Salinger, Catcher in the Rye, p. 4).

The song Bobby McGee referenced above (Kris Kristofferson had so many great lyrics) also has the line**,**

"I'd trade all my tomorrows for just one yesterday." Leonard Cohen sings, **"I can't seem to lose my grip on the past."**

Memory and moving forward cause conflict in the self. Discretion and discernment are all important when we transition ourselves in individuation.

MARWEN

Controlling internal movies means PTSD sufferers can mediate their mind-harrowing circumstances through writing and gain ownership of their minds. This is a planting and harvesting operation. *Welcome to Marwen* is a great movie depicting the great transformational and trans-informational reality of art.

Everyone is an epiphany waiting to happen. The main character has his brain damaged in an assault on him by several men. He picks up the pieces of his life through fantasy. When fantasy and reality start merging he summons the courage to be himself in 'reality'.

 That *Marwen* isn't getting the attention it deserves is symptomatic of an unrepentant society. If you missed Oliver Stone's movie *Snowden* and Michael Moore's last movie, you aren't thinking. Not thinking is preferable for white people who want all this uproar to go away. White people have a lot of mental illness because they want to live in the colonial ego-driven past. I'm white and when I look at Empire and colonialism and selfish exploitation of indigenous people I see the chickens coming home to roost. We need a new open course of action. Those who live by the sword die by the sword.

PLASTICITY

Positive affective-realm orientation is something the schools can't teach objectively. We are talking induction rather than deduction when we are talking creativity. A hybrid idea of art as 'talent' and/or 'categorical knowledge' usurps true art and its style of consciousness. Art school graduates have creativity machined out of them. Dali, Van Gogh and pretty much all the painting geniuses we look back on, could not accept art school and its ramifications in their imaginings. Manet as described earlier opted for creative freedom. It is worrisome how art training would machine their minds, and design their expectations, in specificity-oriented ways. It is the same today. The Arts industry and the schools of art practice a kind of plasticity heresy, constantly turning their backs on originality to pay homage to the mainstream, the superficial. For me Art offers the complexity I need to stay motivated.

Even music choice is something one has, to invite into consciousness. Huxley liked listening to Bach when using mescaline or LSD. Indeed, classical music being lyrics-indeterminate allows infinity of images to take to the air. On LSD you can visualize the notes.

 I cut my teeth on the Moody Blues, the best (to me) LSD music. **I'm paraphrasing from songs etched in my memory.**

From up here you should see the view such a lot of room for me and you

60 foot leaps it's so absurd, I could go on and on

To lie in the meadows and hear the grass sing ... '
was something the Moody Blues got me doing.

Old memory, according to Goswami, projects a cliché reality, a redundant reality, a shadow marching before us into the future.. Most artists I know, 99 percent of them, stick to the old memory route when it comes to creativity. They find a niche. They imitate themselves.

It is creativity by cognitive design. It anticipates and controls according to the likelihood it will sell or not. It eventually becomes increasingly cognitive and less creative.

With each collapse of old memory, the mind is liberated and a proliferation of 'new' super-positions can multiply exponentially. Like a comet, one can catapult through several memory states barely knowing what is going on. These are psychoid precipitates. When Picasso and Dali embarked on a creative voyage they were mindful to leave coherence and safety behind.

A FOOT IN COLD WATER

The finite can defeat us. It gangs up on us. TS Eliot conjures a world he sees as measureable. It is physically sized and finds him wanting. Death is part of it. A slow death.

'A crowd flows over London Bridge, I did not know, death had undone so many.'

Every subway is full of armies of the walking dead.

Prufrock **measures out his life in coffee spoons** waiting to unleash the overwhelming question to an unsuspecting and *disinterested* friend.

Disinterested. Might as well jump.

I saw part of a documentary on suicide a few nights back. A guy was in need of support. He made a pact with himself that he was going to jump off the Golden Gate Bridge... if no one wanted to help him that would be the sign he needed. Like Jerry in *Zoo Story* he had reached a watershed moment. On his way, he broke down on the bus as the magnitude of his soon-to-be suicide bereaved him. He was met with staring vacuous faces and a complete no connect.

He got off at the bridge and for 20 minutes swayed dizzily and paced back and forth crying. People jogged by and walked by. Nobody noticed.

Finally a connection occurred. .

A tourist female asked him to take a couple pictures of her.

She walked away with zero interaction.

After this no-connect he was floored. Nobody fucking cares. It had been confirmed and confirmed again and again.

He jumped.

He surfaced in the water. The coast guard got to him quickly. He suddenly wanted to live. He was busted up big time, his body smashed. He said to God that he would dedicate himself to a meaningful life if he lived. He is following through with that promise.

Life gets many of us down.

In his straight jacket reality J Alfred Prufrock feels the equivalent of **being a pair of ragged claws scuttling ocean floors.**

The Moody Blues echo this—**"Don't you feel small it happens to us all."**

Alice in Wonderland explores the diminutiveness of self. This seems like 'toy' stuff but can be quite dislocating. You can feel like a tiny cell in a big organism. It is all part of the journey. The Mariner had to respect all things great and small. You do too. I do too. I'm often a poor practitioner.

The other side of reality is there for the individuated self. The individuated self can access expansiveness that ties into entropic energy. The truth is, we don't need to be trapped in a fragile mortal coil self. We can soar like eagles. As Jim Morrison would say, 'Break on Through' to the other side. On the other side is the unknown. Being there changes one's outlook. This is metamorphosis, caterpillar to butterfly. Uncertainty becomes an option and opportunity.

BEER CULTURE

As our new provincial premier was raiding cannabis shops opening after legalization (because they weren't owned by the friends of government, who had their own shops), he was promising A BUCK A BEER. There's an old campaign slogan for you. Simultaneously he was shutting down funding for all things French. The old boys are conventionally and conveniently stupid and virtually uneducable because of where they surface on the spectrum. They are inherently lacking self-awareness, empathy and conceptual inter-subjectivity. They are anti education. They will eventually lose their minds but right now they are in power. They play havoc with us. That infringes on us.

This same government that gave away the 407 ETR (toll road) to a private company, has now given the pot industry to private ownership. They are cutting funding to schools and setting up private health care. These are things people should be up in arms about. Most people don't know these politicians are directing big money into private pockets. This is money that could be used for expensive infrastructure. These things infuriate me when I think about them.

Ditto our Federal Government with its disposition to be US controlled in areas of global nonsense including the Ukraine and Venezuela.

But I can't think about them too often. I can't obsess my daily plate with this political crap. To do so poisons the self. Toxicity has to be kept at arms' length.

I need to remind myself, that innumerable other people, in Syria and the Sudan, for example, have finite realities much more self-defeating. To transcend we need to get our minds to a place beyond what is.

This is the perennial trick with plasticity: to keep the head above water. Sinking and swimming are necessarily superimposed in each and every moment. Living and dying are superimposed.

WHAT REASON DO YOU NEED TO DIE?

Bob Geldof's song about one of the very first mass shootings is seemingly a 1000 shootings back now.

"THE SILICON chip inside her head/Gets switched to overload/and nobody's gonna go to school today/she's going to make them stay at home/daddy doesn't understand it/always said she was good as gold."

I Hate Mondays

Often it turns out that something set so and so, off, and they go postal or they catch a bus to the San Francisco Bridge. Tipping points can tip

When social friction reaches apex values a lot of people are going to fly off the handle. A tipping point, or the straw that breaks the camel's back, are precisely how complexes fail and fall. The psyche is a house of cards. The collective mind is riddled with falsely held propositions.

<u>What we reflect about ourselves and about others is the compositional narrative that creates a particular psychodynamic. That psychodynamic is as fragile and vulnerable as our plasticity allows.</u>

I believe it testimonial to my discernment and deliberation skills that I can write what I've written. Most people don't log their ideas in any way shape or form so it makes sense, so they end up losing their way. There is no map, no bread crumbs, no golden thread.

Writing things down is necessary to self-reflect.

I go so far as to suggest most people can't read this stuff. Reading is a dying art. Recognition of truly deep writing is becoming, itself extinct, an anachronism. The ability and capacity is no longer being fired and wired. Everybody is living in the same world massaged by the same thematic structures.

Even to language we bring a lot of cognitive bias and this dismisses outright the notion of a clear see-through language or common denominator logic, said Wittgenstein. You can look at it as thoroughly as linguistically possible. The fact remains, we are embedded, entrenched and ensconced and we can't get around it. Like a fly on sticky paper the stick doesn't stop. We are what we are because the world is what it is.

Our picture, mental picture of the self, is crucial to healing. I'm going to rush what I have to say about Meir Schneider whose work deserves profound study. This mental picture of self is essential to Meir Schneider and is so fundamentally overlooked by everyone else. Meir Schneider believes and advocates: inventing your own healing exercises and developing a feel for yourself. Meir

Schneider and his self-healing books are the best, to my mind. The worst thing you can do is treat yourself with a white lab coat mentality. Your mind-body needs a cheerleader. Schneider's healing is existentially based.

Activity in the empathy network within the limbic system interfaces as close to a person's truth as you can get. The **"maturational settling"** is complicated in its manifest layers, demanding a discovery process as astute as any archeological dig. Maturational settling dupes us into accepting a less spectral reality and a less spectral self. Psychoanalytic enabling creates a field where possibilities materialize.

"The brain in secondary consciousness gravitates toward 'order' and thus, the dynamics in this state are more accurately, (slightly) subcritical. Psychedelics may be therapeutic because they work to normalize pathologically subcritical styles of thought…thereby returning the brain to a more critical mode of operating …. The idea that the brain is closer to criticality in the psychedelic state than in normal waking consciousness has some intuitive appeal as some of the signatures of criticality, such as maximum metastability, avalanche phenomena and hyper sensitivity to perturbation are consistent with the phenomenology of the psychedelic state ….

The psychedelics work to lower repression and facilitate access to the psychoanalytic unconscious," (The Entropic Brain, p. 18).

...

"Phenomena such as spontaneous personal insights and the complex imagery that often plays out in the psychedelic state (Cohen, 1967) and dreaming, may depend on a suspension of repression, enabling cascade-like processes to propagate through the brain," (The Entropic Brain, p. 19).

GOOD MORNING VIETNAM

Robin William's mind was a mess. Despite movies like *Good Will Hunting* and *Dead Poets Society* he continued down the rapids over the edge. These movies could have reached a man willing to be reached; a man that wouldn't feel obligated to tell a joke on an elevator to stuff the gap of time. Philip Seymour Hoffman dramatized an over-the-edge, gas sniffing addict, yet this did not 'touch' him in a discerning way.

The history of now is the history of the failure to be touched, moved, and revolutionized. Those messages we amplify in the self are going to register but less and less as frequencies crunch as into the mass-hysteria which is the future.

I remember one distinct moment during my sojourn in kindergarten, three actually, but each moment is all there is. That which we by-pass goes into the big no-connect. If it's repressed energy it will spring back eventually.

The drugs referenced in *Change Your Mind* and *The Entropic Brain* are drugs that can throw your psyche against the wall and frisk the existential self to the bone. This can turn your life upside down and inside out. If that doesn't freak you out just a little bit, there is something so steadfast, so obsessive-compulsive, so locked-in to certainty, that uncertainty is dead. This is extremely rare.

Life becomes a follow through of your early decisions that congeal in a myelin coated machine brain. This seals one off from input. Psychic energy is finite inside the system of the machine. The machine is a sub-category of mind.

Pauli, Jung, and North-Whitehead agree that psychic energy is no different than molecular energy. People can accept without understanding $E=MC^2$ that equates energy and matter. Psychological energy is the basis of human motivation.

Kids today are brought up on 'Grand Theft Auto' or 'Halo' or the next best thing. That's inherently different than my upbringing which included make-believe, and going outside to play. At school it was about memorizing poetry, like *Along the Line of Smokey Hills*.

Sensibility is desensitized.

Caught between the carrot and the tear gas we have little opportunity to de-comply.

The Entropic Brain paper consolidates a great deal about consciousness. The trouble with Science is, you can dress papers like *The Entropic Brain* up in the best science, pull into the parking lot with 20 pages of referential backup and most scientists won't give it a second thought. They are trapped in their own puppetry, their own puberty.

Since the Manhattan Project, scientists work on teams despite the team mentality being counterproductive in breakthroughs. This is according to Kuhn's breakdown of Scientific Revolutions. Pauli was a lone wolf and creativity was the hallmark of his individuation. When people work on teams the interpersonal reality establishes social hierarchy and establishes levels of discourse. Only the boss can have good ideas. The social norm restricts the Science. Ideas fall into categorical reruns.

Oppenheimer's mother was an artist and his brother a communist. He's one of my heroes because he knew where he was in the big picture. He was at the Alpha and the Omega the beginning of the end.

He said,

"In some sort of crude sense which no vulgarity, no humor no overstatement can quite

extinguish, the physicists have known sin," (Pauli Jung, p. 161).

Oppenheimer was surrounded by military vulgarity. By presenting themselves as Scientists and not as humans Scientists try to abdicate when it comes to moral responsibility. The de-psychologized scientist is simply an awareness-deficient human brain.

Radioactive nucleus was a metaphor for selfhood for Pauli. It's a powerful image. Evolution happens explosively through dimensions personified in the individuation process.

Evil is an option in the human make-up. It's not an option if one is birthing a higher self. Barbarism is backwards, the monkeys heading back to the tree. To do good is the most profound and complex perilous journey. It is the most psychologically satisfying. Despite the central role in civility women have been disparaged by men. The most recent Women's March got zero coverage. Women have to recognize that they are accommodated by men incapable of deep loving feeling.

ZERO COVERAGE ON MOST RECENT WOMEN'S MARCH

"Within the western philosophical tradition, emotions usually have been considered as potentially or actually subversive of knowledge …. Reason rather than emotion has been

regarded as the indispensable faculty for acquiring knowledge …. Reason has been contrasted with emotion, but it has also been associated with the mental, the cultural, the universal, the public and the male, whereas emotion has been associated with the irrational, the physical, the natural, the particular, the private, and of course, the female," (Alison M. Jaggar, 'Love and Knowledge: Emotion in Feminist Epistemology' in Women, Knowledge, and Reality, editors: Ann Garry & Marilyn Pearsall, p. 129).

Samuel Johnson was one of many to chagrin the emotions. He saw the emotions as a gateway to being out of control. This is a convenient myth for someone afraid of confronting the subconscious and the unconscious. Out of control was the very reality of chaos. Lisa Appignanesi in her incredible book, *Sad, Mad and Bad*, profiles insightfully the male-female reality.

This is crucial for humans to grasp the shaping of our history and the prerogatives of our plasticity.

"For males of the time 'It is necessary to maintain that no women at all are fit for them, and that the most eminent women are inferior in mental faculties to the most mediocre of the men on whom those functions at present devolve'," (p. 107). Disintegration of mental life

because of dissociation was attributed more to women. Hysteria was personified in the hysterical woman.

"For Freud 'dissociation or hysteria itself is not due to any constitutional incapacity in the patient for holding mental processes together. Rather, the disintegration of mental life, or dissociation, comes from the psychical process he calls 'repression' – a psychic procedure common in all human development. The exorbitant energy this splitting off of an unwanted part of a past self takes in certain people is what gives patients an air of mental incapacity. He suggests thinking of dissociation as akin to 'preoccupation,' a mental activity which might make any ordinary person seem momentarily less than intelligent," (Appignanesi, p. 163).

"Hysteria is one of those conditions that is reinvented for different times and has cultural malleability almost as dramatic Augustine herself. Elaine Showalter in her *Hystories* has argued that in the 1990'sthe United States has become 'the hot zone of psychogenic diseases,

new and mutating forms of hysteria amplified by modern communications and fin de siècle anxiety'. She lists among these new hysterical syndromes which often convert psychic problems into physical ills or use external sources as evidence for them: chronic fatigue syndrome, multiple personality ..." (Appignanesi, 142).

Today, 'Blue Monday 2019,' an OXFAM report says wealth has never been so concentrated in the history of the human race.

We are falling for the most basic human illusions all over again. Déjà vu. We never learn that you can't build a house on shifting sands, and all that glitters isn't gold. The male species has a tradition of immature plasticity.

American physician, George M. Beard coined the term in 1869 for 'the morbid condition of the exhaustion of the nervous system.

"The condition was one which grew out of the American way of life, with its race for money and power, its excessive pursuit of capital and technological progress. Beard blamed nervous exhaustion on the popular press, the telegraph and steam power, all of which had exasperated

the pressure of modern life. These had made striving, successful men prone to nervous prostration. As for women... incursion into the masculine sphere of intellectual labour...[resulted in] their nervous depletion," (Appignanesi, p. 101-102).

Pauli saw the specific feminine sphere as irreducible in the big picture.

It is a beacon for adjustment. Most males can't recognize the feminine. It scares them to death. The reason many men hate women is because intimacy with them is troubling.

Historically men were seen as incapable of the necessary sympathy and attachment required to raise a child into adulthood.

Transformation is a process in which, according to Pauli, the unconscious takes part. For Jung the confronting of the unconscious is central. For the real artist this is the flow of creativity.

The psyche is a conscious, unconscious whole. The boundaries within its dimensionality are metaphorical. Evolution is **transformation and transformation is the central reality of evolution. There is always a flow of self-realizing processes that never stop.**

Active imagination is fed by thoughts that spontaneously rise to consciousness from the unconscious. The facilitation and practice are essential to self-realization.

Science is censorship-prone because it lacks imagination and it finds an intimate connection with the mind, troubling.

Reflection is a field of continual effort that magnetizes expectation. Automorphism expresses the construction of a system out of itself. We morph by way of plasticity. The system we birth daily is a sub-categorical system that subsumes control and diffuses into a picture of reality. That picture of reality is the picture of the times.

To individuate this process is to birth better systems with better precipitates.

Precipitates can precipitate ad infinitum. The personality becomes inertia within the systems.

Symbolically for Pauli the stakes were high. Formidable thought structures collapsing under the pressure of unconscious forces, is forbidding territory. Being a Scientist, this was doubly difficult to address.

Riddling stability with instability can only be willfully incarnated in a mind willing to find itself, willing to meet itself in a dark alley.

The conscious and the unconscious are one consciousness. Each bleeds into the opposite making the selection of betterment a challenge of action within behaviourism and without.

As Pauli supposed, the repression of unconscious material needs to be addressed. It should be brought to the surface. Repression can surface as mental health trigger issues refuting a person's coherence and undermining the day to day.

"Just as physical perceptions yield precipitates in technical science, so do psychological perceptions find application in life … This can lead to success only if they are actually transposed carefully and conscientiously," (David Lindorff, Jung and Pauli, p. 214).

Pauli was being ultra-careful in transposing himself conscientiously. He knew the nature of the beast. We, the careless, are hard pressed to become conscientious and transposition ourselves towards better plasticity. Pauli needed to be at peace with himself. Like many of us he needed to turn a page.

We need ritual and religious phenomena to bring to the surface the numinous. The belief that Jesus loves me is a numinous belief. Whether White River Apache from Arizona, whose ritual my wife and I shared at a Pow Wow, or self-created, say, featuring your version of reverence for the solstice, the full moon or a tree in the yard ... some metaphorical process is required **to create symbolism of value.**

To connect you to the space that can connect you with the Universe, the self-aware self-conscious universe is the aim of enlightenment. That is in every respect GOD. We need to re-enchant our psyches to even hope to have the range for change.

Most of us see life go by in a blur not knowing what else we can do. Pauli saw Science's lack of capacity for anything other than the typical and the rational, as symptomatic of the world at large. The entrenched Science and its inability to be the least bit flexible freezes its inertia. Humanity is frozen in an apocalyptic pantomime.

I'm not a big psychic phenomena guy. Ouija boards, palm readers and horoscope advocates bring out the sceptic in me. I know people in certain places on the spectrum like Daniel Tammet have incredible off-the-charts ability. Daniel does what, for the rest of us, is impossible. What he doesn't have is 'inter-subjectivity' and the hypothetical conceptual connection. We all need to move on the spectrum to become more evolved. It's not safe to stand still. The brain doesn't like it. To move on the spectrum means you've embodied the lessons in the fibre of your being.

Like Jewel's song about running to stand still, this remains a self-defining reality, **characteristic of this overwhelming and emotionally exhausting blitzkrieg of digital reality:** our all-too-familiar doorstep world where we always are running, but getting nowhere.

An electron can assume certain energy states and its timing for a quantum jump is unpredictable. By shaping where one is in the moment one can fashion better equipment to absorb the moment's needs.

Plasticity can be aroused. That a person's expectations run interference into quantum experiments is a big huge colossal deal. We influence the future by projecting expectations. WE bring the curtain down by collapsing the wave and succumbing to measurement.

BOXING: ROPE-A-DOPE

Mohammed Ali was my inspiration to get into boxing. I was 26-28 years old and about to be divorced and wanted to get into shape. I joined the Orangeville Boxing club managed by a couple army and navy Brits who also ran the Academy for Dogs north of Orangeville on Highway 10. Currently, 42 years later, it is dilapidated and up for sale. Not too far into my boxing career I took LSD and settled in for some fun. It was Friday night.

At 9 pm the boxing coach phoned. The army guy was the main coach and he was inquiring to see if I would take Joe Alexander's fight as he couldn't make weight. I agreed before thinking it through. Real 'fights' don't come up that often.

The last time I saw Joe (looking back now) he was driving up Broadway in Orangeville in a Porsche with a beautiful blonde beside him. This was years after he couldn't make weight.

Joe was from Alton, his family farm on the outskirts. He was a blacksmith. One summer I drove a Euclid in the gravel pit where his brother worked.

I said yes to the fight and of course never slept a wink. On LSD you can't sleep. You close your eyes and the fun goes on.

On that fight card was the flashy Nicky Furlano, Benny Guindon and three New York State Golden Gloves Finalists.

Benny Guindon was leader of the Satan's Choice and the Choice saddled up the best seats in the house. It was a big arena in Bramalea (Brampton), Saturday night with a lot of people. I was shaking in my boots. The Orangeville newspaper said I picked myself up off the canvas and went on to win the fight. When I read this I realized, I didn't even remember being knocked down. The guy I fought was from Leamington, Ontario..

I mention this because LSD is a great physical training experience. It clears the way subconsciously, so one wants to do better.

Threatened by divorce I typically and stupidly took refuge in my masculine side.

One of Jung and Pauli's mainframe ideas: "THE COMPLEX USURPS THE SOVREIGNTY OF THE EGO." This is fundamental understanding, strategic to understanding how social forces contour mindscape, eclipsing the individual's efforts to consummate otherwise.

When I was in high school it was actually a thing you said to people: What, you got a *complex*?

We are a complex of thoughts, a package with a certain design. That design is usually a default mechanism schooled in repressing emotional and unconscious needs. It is the script of Normalization.

That's why letting go of the ego in a drug experience, or in real time divorce or life situation, is often impossibly difficult.

Divorce sent me into a downward spiral.

Many people suffer a major dislocation when they break up. A person you have invested in emotionally and vice versa and now it is zero.

We live in a time of perpetual disorientation of the psyche. This is the age of anxiety and the overwhelm. The 'overwhelm' is the monster to which we sacrifice ourselves and our children.

PRECIPITATION

The autonomous energy of the subconscious has infused art and literature with its power. When plasticity percolates, psychoids start looking for somewhere to go.

Precipitates are everywhere. There is infinity of precipitates. Knock and the door shall be open. The high priests of art and of science don't go there. They are content with the world as it is. The autonomous unconscious poses a threat to their well-organized and predisposed psyche. They are trapped in a physical world of pre-cognition longitude and latitude. A painted ship on a painted ocean suits them fine.

Conscientious transformation is the very stuff of plasticity. This is because it involves the most pivotal and life-changing 'critical' aspects of self. When conscience walks through the valley of the shadow of death, courage is the blossom and the prerequisite. Creativity always comes down to the first step. The first step involves waving goodbye to the shoreline.

WORLD CLASS PAINTER AND THE SYNCHRONOUS ENCOUNTER

Events of compression and responsibility have a great deal of power to distort our bearing, dysfunction-alize our actions. When I see this happening to someone I want to intervene. Of course I could be interpreting things incorrectly. Sometimes a person can demand too much from the self. The more decent a person is the more trapped in doing the decent thing.

Because of a recent couple of narrative demands on this painter's plasticity management, I felt compelled to speak up and probably shouldn't have. For some dumbass reason (intuition) I thought there was compressed energy that needed to be released. Somewhere I 'felt' his current project was contradistinctive to what I felt he needed. Maybe I was right, maybe not. I thought he needed deep breathing not squinting out detail.

PAINTED SHIP ON A PAINTED OCEAN

"I had killed the bird that made the breeze to blow. Day after day, day after day we [were] stuck, nor breath nor motions as idle as a painted ship upon a painted ocean …. For the sky and the sea, and the sea and the sky. Lay dead like a load on my weary eye and the dead were at my feet."

The subject mariner of the poem was on a ship, a large sailing vessel. He and the crew were doing okay till the mariner shot with his bow, an albatross .The sailors knew this was a bad thing to do. The Albatross like Noah's dove was a sign.

In folklore, the breeze would no longer blow the breeze-bringing albatross was dead. Sure enough. The ship was stationary; there was no wind for the sails. Days grew into weeks.

Coleridge was using a metaphor for the creative spirit, a wind that blows through the proverbial Aeolian harp to release the music. Without the breeze flow would stop and the music would cease.

For the mariner it was a gruesome acid-like trip. The crew died and became skeletal. Only when the mariner respected all things great and small did the ship move.

The painted ship on a painted ocean was a symbol of no wind and metaphorically no creativity. For what it's worth, the coincidence that the painter I met was painting a ship on the ocean was synchronous sign.

NEUROGENESIS

But here is the symbolic crux of the matter. This book is front to back an exercise in synchronicity. So why not this?

Entering the age bracket of the sixties with questions of mortality confronting him personally, on so many fronts, I felt it my job to intervene and save him. Save him from a plasticity event for which the timing was not right. Impolitely I think (after all I'm an x-variable stranger) I tried to tell a world class painter what to paint.

Actually, I was telling him what not to paint. I felt it might bring about an anger-repression polarity, a scheduling of energy, because he was demanding a lot of himself, after a lot had been demanded of him.

Neurogenesis

By stopping himself from doing something different than what he was doing, he was creating 'scheduling' precedence. That precedence might play tricks with future creative access.

This painter is a man of seemingly impeccable character with a deeper humanity than I possess.

Am I a jealous painter with a chip on my shoulder or someone pointing to a 'higher way'?

That's the question. And it's always the question and always will be:

How do we manage our plasticity?????? What are the events that liberate us most resoundingly from maturational settling?

My wife questions me as to my inclusion of this encounter. To me there is an intra-psychic world and an ultra-psychic world. Usually I'm dumb as the next guy in accessing such frequencies. There are wave formations that carry me into territory where synchronicity and intuition become important. Just as Jung and Pauli thought self-scrutiny most important and strategic so to, I try to negotiate its importance in real time. For Jung it was important to put the self in the big picture with the big backdrop. Are you, today right now a victim, a hero, a villain? Metaphorical thinking becomes part of the intuition going forward. It is a surreal plot on its own frequency. This helps with daily strategy of being. So an encounter with world class painter became both real and unreal, both in circumstances and without. There is a lot more synchronicity in this encounter than I've profiled but enough to make it unusual.

At every turn, in each and every moment, the brain is being PLASTICIZED for better or for worse. Nobody, not even world class painters are off the hook. Prince Philip just crashed his Landover into a small car with two women and a baby. Royalty isn't off the hook. Philip can be rigid and stubborn and stupid like anyone else.

For most of those aging comfortably, the comfy blanket grows into the deep sleep.

What Pauli knew and what Kurt Cobain dreaded was the burn out that attacks the life-size adult. People's dreams fade and get lost in their own finger prints. The masterpiece remains unsigned.

Most see aging as a necessary part of aging so the mind is programmed. Its effects are prime time and the pharmaceuticals are shoving their ads about infinite decrepitude in our faces.

In *the Brain That Changes Itself*, Doidge shows how the brain can teach stroke victims to regain physical function. But we don't have to sift through the thousands of cases of those types of physical manifestation to believe in the power of mentalness.

It's fact. In Neuroscience it is everywhere apparent.

In writing about synchronicity and Pauli's dreams, the frequency of synchronous events has interestingly escalated. To top it off, my wife was showing me a linguistic program on the computer.

The beauty of synchronicity is in its improbability. Because I was finishing off this entropic brain writing, she put that into a phrase for the French-English translation. This came up in reference to artist, Pierre Bismuth. He refers to his art as exploring:

"Constant transformations and spontaneous change, an entropic release of excess energy in a system that gradually discloses its paradoxes."

Once again, somebody said it better than I ever could and it fell into my lap. This is an artistic scientific explanation by an artist, in keeping with consummate understandings, involving the entropic brain reality. Paradox is important and it is everywhere.

It is the condition of free-flow that characterizes the creative engagement. The precipitates are magnetized and perturbation is non-local and non-causal -- so get over it.

Let us remember in closing that the unsought for organization of rigidity, is a simple by-product of turnstile, socialization. The results are complex. In education, art, and science the dubious results become manifest and are manifest.

Indeed, the most threatening style of breakdown is to find oneself embedded in conformity so your mind is indistinguishable from the herd. Being one of the lemmings is reflective of a desire to avoid confrontation between the known and the unknown. The lemmings are the inertia portrait mentioned earlier; the snapshot of a life sentence frozen in psychological space. Like a deer in the headlights we are in the headlights of an unknown future.

Gravity articulates matter. In this sense a planet in orbit finds a relationship with gravity that articulates orbit and even the planet's shape over time. With humans, psychological gravity articulates our bodies: posture, gait, weight and metabolism, and heart strength. If you get a promotion or demotion at work, your 'system' responds by absorbing stress systematically. If you break up with a long-time lover, the shape of the disengagement will be telling in the body. Everything has to be disentangled. Psychic translations of circumstances play havoc with our navigational opportunities. Who we are and why we are this way become issues. It all registers and polarities are refined.

THE BODY ELECTRIC

The electric cell with its central negative zone, an inner positive zone, cell membrane, outer positive zone and outer negative zone are tiny of course and complex. Transmembrane receptor proteins, receptor antennae, etc., negotiate the confluences up and down the system.

Negotiating gap zones articulate energy pronouncements in a holistic reality not readily or ever learned in the **atomization of detail.**

Science is good at atomizing details and missing the boat. Looking protein or psychology down, that is the question.

"Taken together, the similar large-scale topology of the metabolic and the protein interaction networks indicate the existence of a high degree of harmony in the cell's architecture," (Albert-Laszlo Barabasi, Linked, p. 189).

The manifestations of your physical nature reflect colossal interactions at every level. Harmony is disrupted and those disruptions can be polarized. The body becomes entrenched as a permanently organized system. The organization of the system, too often rejects complexity in favour of simplicity. You like to think this thought over and over again. The mind expedites that thought. Simplicity is easy to understand. We get simplicity. We want to get it. Human being after human being willingly satisfies the 'all' for an evidentiary-prone life, based on imposed expectations and unfortunate criteria. We've been warned by Mythology and Religion, by Psychiatry and Poetry. And we have been warned by scientists willing to run a different race, a race differentiated from the pack. Such a scientist was Wolfgang Pauli.

We necessarily and unavoidably fire and wire a new brain every day. That's a life sentence. In most people that brain is the same brain and the brain's structure becomes undifferentiated and increasingly difficult to differentiate. Eventually the energy to run a closed system is closed system energy. It runs down. A failure to embolden neuroplasticity and neurogenesis is a failure of untold consequence. Those consequences result in dissociation which can take many different forms as reflected in the mental health spectrum.

This is simply because conformity, consistency and coherence seem antithetical to entropy. Unfortunately a lot of people never get to this realization except perhaps for one microsecond when they stand looking in the mirror not knowing who they are or how they got there. Conformity erases the self.

In the end it all goes down this way: creativity is antithetical to how schools deliver information. We get faster at retrieving information and in parallel we misadjust to those essence-sustaining items we need to survive. There are prerequisites that come with the anatomy of the human mind: each and every mind whether African, Chinese, Russian, or whatever. There are tendencies within a culture. Plasticity is plastic. Culture plasticizes. Any religious garb or costume diminishes one's role in individuation. You march under a flag which creates self-determinism. Or you are child to the universe.

Most Whites are not living in colonial luxury. Many are below the poverty line. On any street most families are deeply fractured. It's the rich and greedy white people who own the banks and giant media outlets who are the barbarians. Slime-balls in suits with sandbox intellects.

But they too can migrate their firing and wiring. To not do this and be in possession of a human brain is sacrilege.

Plasticity is for all. Self-realization and individuation is what the truly responsible brain needs to be about. Art is a kind of voyeurism. First the artist looks deep inside and tries to process the subconscious flow and bring this particular alignment into view. This is where value is assigned on one side of the fence or the other. To piece something together that is new is neurogenesis in action. It feels like it comes as inspiration because it does. Where does neurogenesis come from if not outside the individual? It exists as a precondition of the universe.

Think of how hard it is to create something never before created like the Dadaists and Surrealists did! By doing this you arouse into being different ways of understanding your own mind in action.

Art groups and curators world-wide are merely educated creatures. Their only litmus is in their paper certificate of proficiency in all things not creative. They, by their training, miss the boat in third eye activity.

The candy-ass bourgeois are on the ramparts defending the superficial and their gala evenings of self-congratulatory indulgence. They are pretenders. They are posers. They don't know their ass from their elbow when it comes to neuroscience, and the art of creativity.

Art is jurisdiction of the creative impulse. It finds you if you are looking for it. The viewer sees the artist as caught in the act, an act of the imagination. From that there is everything to learn.

Where does this leave us?

It leaves us with a lot of people estranged from themselves.

Assembly-line doctors depersonalize their mentality with every de-personalized personal encounter. You cannot under normalized circumstance re-personalize the self. The same goes for cops and people working in abattoirs and collection agencies.

These doctors will someday lose their minds; their methodology not up for aging. My friend's doctor of 20-some years died 4 weeks after he retired. The problem is in function-driven personalities. They are latent obsessive-compulsive passive-aggressive personalities at a complete loss without function to order the day. You are capacitating or incapacitating daily. Incapacitation leads to unused aspects. You think you can call these things back but you can't.

A book like *Change Your Mind* points out the problematic nature of change. The fact is we become cognitively reconciled. Our switching mechanisms become layered in typical use and non-use strategies. Cognitive reconciliation is tantamount to biochemical resolution. You don't change overnight and in most cases no changes are possible. (TS Eliot refers to this opportunity as **more distant than a fading star**.)

All memory is not the same. One memory is trivial pursuits based. The Jeopardy show profiles a certain type of fact that has little leverage within the mentality as such. My wife never loses when playing me at Jeopardy. This has given her a false sense of superiority.

Another memory entirely, catalogues our narrative moments of consequence, of love and betrayal, of birth and death. As part of a more generalized confederation of dunces our mentality suffers and needs rigorous protection. It needs pampering, attention and deep consideration.

We are fragile creatures susceptible to bullshit and every gimmick, and every investment opportunity and every thought in between.

An a-ha moment is a liberation from typical maturational reality and typical memory constraints. It thrusts us into an archetypal relationship with 'muse,' inspiration, and transcendence. There we get knocked off the donkey and onto a new path. The new path births the new. In the end the unconscious self needs to be confronted. There is no slaying of demons. We incorporate our demons into a balanced complexity. Balance between old and new, death and life is where the zero self can manifest exponentially. The role of the magician warrior is to balance both worlds.

When I look back in life some odd things surface confirming the two worlds.

Once upon a time the couple who was part of the bad acid trip invited us to a New Year's party. He was making big bucks with Ampex at the time. I was at York University at the time. Again I remember nothing of that night except one thing. This was in an industrial party centre or something in Toronto but not downtown. Probably North York.

As we departed and walked away not long after midnight, there was noise and commotion behind us at the door. This was 20-30 feet behind us. We were crossing the parking lot to get to the car watching an oil slick pooling beneath the street lamps. Some party-ers were leaving in a gust of noise. It wasn't too cold for New Years. It wasn't snowing.

As we looked back at the commotion, a tall man was descending the steps. In each hand he had a triangular party hat. On his head he had a similar hat. As he was coming down the steps it was like he was trying to keep his arms outstretched and keep his balance something somebody drunk or on drugs might do. For months if not years that scene was etched in my mind. For me it had all the earmarking of a sign. A sign I never could figure out.

Eventually the image slipped out of mind till I wrote those words about the magician-guy, who I began to see as Merlin balancing two worlds. This New Year's image had come back to me from out of nowhere.

We live in a land of echolation where frequencies are boundaries. This is convenient for our sensory system. We are suspended in this animation, always favouring precognition and prejudice. One is systemic in how we do what we do and this is the monster that eats us alive. Much of white culture is living in a bubble.

Patrick Chan was never embraced like Elvis Stojko or Kurt Browning. The Chinese have recently charged Canada of having double standards. I've taught a hundred or more Chinese students. They were all polite. Desmond Tutu, when he visited the Canadian indigenous people, pointed out that Canada had its own apartheid. There are a lot of aspects of the American South that are Canadian.

There are none so blind, as those who refuse to see.

I'LL CALL YOU ON YOUR CELLPHONE

Bell Canada is going collect a lot of money at the end of this month under the auspices of LET'S TALK. They have collected tens of millions since the advent of Let's Talk. In trying to find out where the money goes, I have been refuted. Apparently, people can apply for 5000 dollar grants but I could find no such grants that were granted. 5000 bucks is a paltry sum anyhow. I believe Bell may be conning people out of cash. Why not show us the initiatives? Surely by now, years into this Let's Talk,, they would have profiles of all the good accomplished. Has their revenue gone up because of Let's Talk. Instead they rerun the stuff from the beginning with the original Bell Let's Talk. White men speak with forked tongue.

Recently Bell and Roger's have been exposed in unfair sales and billing practices. Of course they own the Media outlets so coverage has been minimal.

For me, Bell is the most stressful company to deal with. They stonewall or misdirect. If a company that causes stress amongst thousands if not hundreds of thousands of customers gets a pat on the back for addressing mental health while sticking it to us...Come on Man......

Show Us The Money, Ma Bell

This is so Canadian. MADD, a few years ago, was exposed as using up to 90 percent of the charitable donations for their own paychecks. We have sinned and come short of the Glory of God.

The Canadian banks make billions in profits yearly. The Royal Bank, I believe, had a billion dollars of profit in 3 months. This is profit: this isn't 'net'. We are a society that believes in the mighty dollar and this is an epic mistake.

Another synchronicity: I'm starting to read Eben Alexander's book: LIVING IN A MINDFUL UNIVERSE. I'm throwing some quotes at you from that book.

"A convergence of understanding about our approach to science, our universe, and ourselves is the only way forward. For those with the most open minds, this is where science finds itself now, in the early 21st century, as it finally comes closer to some understanding of the depths of the mind-body debate. This fascinating investigation into the fundamental nature of reality is directly relevant to us all," (49).

Schopenhauer said, "The discovery of truth is prevented more effectively, not by the false appearance of things present and which mislead into error, not directly by weakness of the reasoning powers, but by preconceived opinion, by prejudice," (p. 46).

> **"I was absolutely bound to share with the world that our conventional understanding of reality as explained by materialist science was completely false and misleading,"** (p. 26).

There are immediate implications of plasticity we have to embrace. My wife brought home a developing situation in the schools that was an item in the news.

I'm condensing this, way farther than I should, just to throw it in stark relief, a scene repeated daily in local schools. A seven year old Autistic boy has been swearing in class and assaulting kids and teachers. The Board has sent him home. His mother and father are exasperated. They want inclusion, and understandably, see it as their constitutional right.

The boy has lots of energy and has even attacked the mother. When I was teaching in Meadowvale at Meadowvale Secondary guys from the football team would be hired to look after an autistic boy who was violent and liked to smash things.

My wife's last time in the classroom featured a repeated scenario where a student with ADHD spoke to her aggressively and took over the class. He was doing what he was compelled to, to satisfy his attention span.

FINE.

I am the Empathy guy. We need to care for these kids who are a puppet on the string to dysfunction-alized fire and wiring.

BUT - -

In the meantime, back at the ranch as they used to say in the old days, kids still leave for school expecting to be educated. However, every day there are classroom fireworks and tension prevails. A kid in this sort of classroom is swimming against the current to grasp onto learning. It ain't going to happen. Our schools are dishevelled and our teachers under threat. And parents whose children deserve inclusion because that's what civilized countries are about, are getting ready to sue.

There is no answer. Somewhere someone isn't being accommodated. It's the facts of life. There are so many depressed kids in school, bi-polar kids, ADHD kids, Autistic and Asperger's kids we need something different. I've explained elsewhere what I believe Autistics need in education entails individuation and subjectivism. This involves lots of videotaping, particularly expressions, in action.

It is getting outdoors as often as possible that helps a kid focus far-range.

Anyhow, I'm wasting my time. My efforts to arouse interest in the Autism community have made me deflect from an attempt to get this across. Similarly I suspect my idea would not pass the litmus test of the precognitive mannerisms and expectations invisibly at work in our collective interpretive awareness. They are too far beyond the frame-up of the system.

I leave you with this quotation by Albert Einstein and this is why schools have to self-correct accordingly:

"We cannot solve our problems with the same thinking we used when we created them," Albert Einstein as quoted in (Eben Alexander, Living in a Mindful Universe, p. 59).

I am a white person and it troubles me that rich white people are destroying civilization with their greed. It is horrible to load this weight on one's mind going forward, the idea that the future is irrevocably broken and we're caught in endgame. That poor white people are the victims of greedy white people is disparaging. Ditto for other victimized races. There is no need for it. The ape just can't get enough of aping himself. His nurse maid is habit and patriarchy is a destiny too implanted.

Last night my wife and I saw the movie, *Green Book*. It's early January 2019 and it is way below zero. I'm trying to embrace winter but it is cold-hearted.

Green Book is about a virtuoso black man: Don Shirley. Shirley spoke 8 languages. He had doctorate degrees in music, liturgy and psychology. He was a composer. In *Green Book* he decides to tour the Southern States. His white driver has to find occasionally a motel where the Coloured folk can stay. This world famous rich composer that Igor Stravinsky praised had to hobo down because of skin colour.

White people would welcome him warmly into their establishments, shake his hand, pat him on the back, and send him to the outhouse. Whether this was a truthful or fictionalized account it speaks the truth about white people and civil rights. Every white person should see how this movie unfolds, how this white Italian and this gifted black man become friends.

What we forget is what is crucial and important. Incrementally people lose their minds. And they do it because of false motifs. Religion and Mythology have mapped out the typical pitfalls.

Pauli's long road to Damascus was about uprooting falsifying motifs. It was about squaring the arithmetic. And recognizing what's in and outside the box. It's about looking in the mirror and gauging one's ability to walk on water, whoever the critics and however mainstream those grounded in the pre-emptive and prescriptive.

We, as white people have had the rug pulled out from under us. To pretend it is still there, that the world is our doorstep and our doormat is no longer workable. To blame what is happening on skin colour or race is mental midgetry.

These two quotes, one from Orwell's *Animal Farm* and one from *Adbusters* magazine are a couple things for our collective consciousness, yours and mine to ponder. This *Animal Farm* quotation illustrates metaphorically and literally what we are up against:

"Sometimes the older ones among them racked their dim memories and tried to determine whether in the early days of the rebellion, when Jones' expulsion was still recent, things had been better or worse than now …. Squealer's lists of figures which invariably demonstrated that everything was getting better and better ….

They never lost, even for an instant, their sense of honour and privilege of being members Animal Farm …. And when they heard the gun booming and saw the green flag fluttering at the masthead, their hearts swelled with imperishable pride ….

Benjamin felt a nose nuzzling at his shoulder. He looked around. It was Clover. Her old eyes looked dimmer than ever. Without saying

anything she tugged gently at his mane and led him around to the end of big barn where the seven commandments were written. For a minute or two they stood gazing at the tarred wall with its white lettering ... Benjamin read out to her what was written on the wall. There was nothing there now except a single commandment. It ran: ALL ANIMALS ARE EQUAL BUT SOME ANIMALS ARE MORE EQUAL THAN OTHERS. After that it did not seem strange when next day the pigs who were supervising the work of the farm all carried whips in their trotters. It did not seem strange to learn that the pigs had bought themselves a wireless set were arranging to install a telephone, and had taken out subscriptions to JOHN BULL, TIT-BITS, and the DAILY MIRROR," (George Orwell, Animal Farm, p. 87-90).

The way I see it, nobody is coming to help, no cavalry, no deux ex machina, no bubble gum opera, no man in a mask. We are on our own, decked out in squabbles immersed in discourse acting out our unconscious disarray.

"No-one is coming to save you, Comrade.

There is no revolution on the horizon, there is no party, there is no grand idea that will finally awaken humanity to its potential and free us from our chains. There is no vanguard, no purpose, no secret method we can use to magically make the powerful resign themselves to the fate of ordinary existence. There have been pretenders. There are priests and pimps and false gods that call on you to worship them. They will give you immortal 'sciences' and identities, they will assure you if enough people just donned the uniform or spoke the right words everything would be okay …. They, so wise, say they will 'wait for the people to rise.' The people have risen and been crushed. Occupy failed, Standing Rock failed. All that's left is you and me. Everybody is sure change is right around the corner, that divine powers will steer us the right way. Everybody if sure time is on our side, that the good ones will always win and that things can't hold out much longer," (Dr. Bones, Adbusters, Vol. 25, No. 4).

XXXXXXXXXXXXXXXXX

When the worker animals took over from farmer Jones the dictator who exploited them cruelly and uncaringly, they had little idea that power-mongers of their own would turn the revolution upside down. The pigs grabbed the apples, raised guard dogs and slept in beds. White on White violence is the most ignored violence. It is subtle but exacting. What we are doing to each other's mindscapes is irrevocable damage.

What we need to do to save ourselves is set better normalization criteria in motion. Education needs to address the complex needs of the multiple dimension human being. Neurogenesis and creativity are the most significant criteria objectives going forward into the uncertain future. We need to be more honest and more aware.

At the beginning I talked a little about the Fountain of Youth and little about Wittgenstein.

In his biography of Wittgenstein Ray Monk (Ludwig Wittgenstein, The Duty of Genius) talks on page 143 about things that can't be put into words. He quotes Wittgenstein regarding relinquishing 'the ordinary way of considering things'. That means dropping the questions that corroborate experience and reduce it to a label.

Monk quotes Spinoza's statement to show where Wittgenstein's thinking was coming from.

"The mind is eternal insofar as it conceives things from the standpoint of eternity"

The fountain of youth is the process by which we eternalize the now. Indeed eternalizing the now is what forever is all about.

Show me the magic.

Vivamus ut viximus

Let us be truthful to one another.

DAVID COURTNEY, 2019

Neurogenesis

Manufactured by Amazon.ca
Bolton, ON

34776569R00157